THE KILLING OF TUPAC SHAKUR

The **KILLING**of TUPAC SHAKUR

Cathy Scott

Plexus, London

All rights reserved including the right of
reproduction in whole or in part in any form
Copyright © 1997, 1999 by Cathy Scott
Published by Plexus Publishing Limited
55a Clapham Common Southside
London SW4 9BX
First Printing 1999

British Library Cataloguing in Publication Data

Scott, Cathy
  The killing of Tupac Shakur
  1. Shakur, Tupac 2. Rap musicians - United States - Biography
  I. Title
  782.4'2'1649'092

ISBN 0 85965 273 4

Published by arrangement with
Huntington Press, Las Vegas, Nevada

Cover photo: Corjuni/Katz/Outline (front cover)
Aaron Mayes (author photo)
Cover design: Philip Gambrill
Printed in Great Britain
by J. W. Arrowsmith Ltd

10 9 8 7 6 5 4 3 2

To the memory of my grandmother, Esther Rose (1901-1990), a Carmel, California artist with an intellect far too early for her time.

And to the grieving mothers who have lost their sons to gangsta violence: My sincere sympathies to you all as you struggle to make sense of their deaths.

ACKNOWLEDGEMENTS

Many people (and a loyal Siamese) stood by me as I finished this manuscript. In the words of Tupac Shakur, "You are appreciated."

First, to Anthony Curtis and Deke Castleman at Huntington Press and their entire staff (especially Jason Cox, Bethany Coffey, and Len Cipkins) for believing that the killing of Tupac Shakur was a Las Vegas story that needed to be told and that I was the one to tell it, and for their incredible editing, focus, and dedication to the manuscript—you steered me and the words in the right directions and made it better.

To the Las Vegas Metropolitan Police Department, notably Lieutenant Wayne Petersen and Detectives Brent Becker and Mike Franks, for their interviews, but especially Sergeant Kevin Manning for putting up with my many questions and allowing me to flesh out the story.

To the *Las Vegas Sun* for its support and for giving me time off to work on the manuscript, particularly City Editor (and my boss) Geoff Schumacher; to the *Sun's* daytime copy desk—Rob Langrell, Linda Wrzesinski, and Sal DeFilippo—for their endless good humor and encouragement; and to photographers Steve Marcus, Marsh Starks, and Aaron Mayes for their images.

A special thanks to the *Sun's* online department (www.lasvegassun.com) for their innovation in packaging the daily Tupac stories; I especially thank Jennifer Whitehair for her hard work.

To my attorney Vickie Pynchon for her legal counseling and a lifetime friendship that began in grade school where we had early aspirations in "Sisters of the Pen" of one day becoming writers.

To Kevin Doty, Esq. and Kent Lauer with the Nevada

Press Association for their advice.

To my sources, who for obvious reasons I won't name. And to one in particular—you know who you are—a thank you from the heart for reading every word I write, for understanding the role of a journalist, and for being my friend.

To my fellow newswomen and newsmen, allies and sterling journalists all: Kevin Powell for his sensitive description of the man, not just the rapper; Tonya Pendleton for her insights into the world of rap; Rachael Levy for forever being the devil's advocate and making me a better reporter; Charlene Fern for forcing style, style, style at my first daily paper; Karen Colterman for her soft criticism; columnist John L. Smith for his confidence in my abilities; cartoonist Mike Smith for his steadfast support; Muriel Stevens for her sound literary advice; Myram Borders for her Las Vegas history; "Kayaking" Steve Waterstrat for his friendship; Teresa Hinds for listening and for loaning me author Bill Moody—her fiance—so I could pick his brain; and the *Sun's* executive editor, former Nevada Governor Mike O'Callaghan, for believing in me—for that I am grateful.

To my family, most of whom were long-distance boosters: my son Raymond Somers Jr. for his never-failing encouragement and blessings; my mother, writer Eileen Rose Busby, who taught me I could achieve whatever in life I chose; my father James Melvin Scott, whose writing of his own book at 85 spurred me on to pen my own; my big brothers, Jon Scott for his continued faith and Michael Scott for his scholarly and brotherly advice; my sister Sally Scott for passing on her love of literature to me; and my twin sister Cordelia Mendoza who has always been there for me.

To my cousin Brian Corey for hauling my gear into the Grand Canyon, so I could make it out and finish this book.

To Tupac Amaru Shakur (R.I. P.).

And, finally, my gratitude to a Grossmont College instructor whose name I no longer know and who is still unaware of the impact he had on a sophomore in his creative writing class when he told her she had talent.

TABLE OF CONTENTS

AUTHOR'S NOTE

I've endeavored to uncover the truth about the killing of Tupac Shakur. Perhaps no one will ever know for sure who pulled the trigger—except the killer or killers. What I do know is this: someone has gotten away with murder.

I'm not trying to solve the murder case; from the start, my goal has been to separate fact from fiction in this extremely high-profile case. Much of the information I've gathered and presented here has never been published before. In some cases, I've identified errors previously reported and replaced them with the facts as I've learned them and know them to be true.

This book is based on interviews, research, and observations during my ten months covering this story. I've gleaned information from a prodigious paper trail, including county, police, and legal documents and records. I've perused hundreds of newspaper and magazine articles, some of which were not always accurate. In piecing together the events of September 7, 1996, and their continuing aftermath, I have diligently and painstakingly checked and rechecked the facts. I'm a police reporter by trade; it's my job to get the words right.

I've interviewed scores of people about this murder. Nearly 100 are cited. Some of my sources provided background information only and their names are not included in the text. Although I've had many conversations with Shakur family members and their attorneys, agents, and assistants, Tupac's mother, Afeni Shakur, decided at the last minute not to submit to an interview. Instead, I've included the few published comments she has made since Tupac's death. I'm told by her attorney that she is still grieving and has difficulty discussing her son, especially his murder.

The Las Vegas Metropolitan Police Department, known as Metro, has been mostly forthcoming. In the past, the Las Vegas cops have been notoriously tight-lipped—all the way up to the highest levels. Long-term sheriff, John Moran, consistently refused to talk to reporters; even when he retired in December 1994, Moran declined to give a final interview, standing his ground and closing his door to the press one last time.

That attitude has carried over into the current administration of Sheriff Jerry Keller. Although Keller talks to the media, he becomes openly indignant and critical of reporters when the questions get too tough.

And though homicide detectives and others close to the Tupac Shakur case were understandably reluctant at times to discuss certain aspects of the case, they eventually provided enough details to allow me to construct an accurate portrayal of the events surrounding the criminal investigation.

Metro officers, however, drew the line when it came to speaking with out-of-town reporters, purposely fielding questions only from local journalists, whom they knew. As a result, the newsroom at the *Las Vegas Sun* where I work received calls from dozens of reporters from all over the country who had been stonewalled by the Las Vegas police.

The world was watching the Tupac Shakur case unfold daily and the *Las Vegas Sun* was ahead of the curveball each day, beating the competition in the quest to break the news. After all, this was *our* town and *our* story. We weren't about to let the national papers gobble it up and take it away from us. During the first week, my paper assigned three reporters to the case, but the shooting investigation was all mine.

My pursuit of this story turned up a fascinating and convoluted sequence of events surrounding not just the shooting, but Tupac himself and the world in which he lived. I piece them together in the pages that follow.

This book is not intended as an endorsement of the gangsta lifestyle; it's an accounting of the events. The language is raw and the drama could have come straight from the most violent movie. It didn't. This is not fiction. The players in these pages are real. This is a true, violent, and sad story of an unsolved crime, based on the facts. It's the story of the killing of Tupac Shakur.

1

THE KILLING OF TUPAC SHAKUR

The championship boxing match between heavyweights Mike Tyson and Bruce Seldon on the night of Saturday, September 7, 1996, packed Las Vegas with fight fans, including celebrities from every medium. Las Vegas nears peak capacity almost every weekend of the year, but this fight, a premier event, sold out all the hotel and motel rooms in the city and gridlocked the Las Vegas Strip.

It would turn out to be a deadly fight night.

Vegas is famous for its boxing events, which have been magnets for high-spending action since Sonny Liston's first-round knock-out of Floyd Patterson in 1963. Mohammed Ali, Larry Holmes, Roberto Duran, Sugar Ray Leonard, Evander Holyfield, Mike Tyson, and a long list of great fighters have turned Las Vegas into a world-class mecca for boxing. Heavyweight bouts traditionally wrap Las Vegas in an electrifying atmosphere that rarely materializes during other events. They can gross more than $100 million, especially when Tyson fights.

On this day, Mike Tyson was expected to win back the heavyweight championship he'd lost years earlier to Buster Douglas, and high rollers flocked to the desert at the invitation of the casinos to attend the fight as an opening act to a weekend of partying and gambling.

"Nothing brings customers to Las Vegas like major heavyweight boxing, and Mike Tyson is the biggest draw in boxing, so it's a big special event for this town," commented Bill Doak, marketing director for the MGM Grand Hotel and Casino, where the fight was held.

"The exposure Las Vegas will get will be incalculable in terms of media exposure," effused Rob Powers, spokesman for the Las Vegas Convention and Visitors Authority.

Everything at the MGM Grand spelled H-O-L-L-Y-W-O-O-D, from its upscale stores and gourmet restaurants to the red-carpeted Studio Walk leading to the MGM Grand Garden where two fights—one a boxing match, the other a brawl—would take place that night.

Tupac (pronounced "TOO-pock") Shakur, one of the most notorious emcees on the rap music scene, was among the many celebrities who assembled at the MGM Grand for the fight. It wasn't the first time Tupac had come to town for a heavyweight bout. Six months earlier, Tupac and fellow gangsta rap artist Snoop Doggy Dogg had attended the Mike Tyson-Frank Bruno fight at Caesars Palace.

Also in town for the Tyson-Seldon match-up were the Rev. Jesse Jackson, an avid fight fan and a familiar face in Las Vegas on fight weekends, as well as rapper M.C. Hammer, television star Roseanne, basketball player Gary Payton, and hip-hop's Too Short and Run-DMC.

They, along with 16,000 spectators in the arena and millions more sitting glued to the pay-per-view cable channel, watched as Tyson dismantled Seldon in exactly 109 seconds. The spectators barely had time to settle into their seats before they found themselves getting up again and filing back out of the arena. Some spectators remained in their seats for a few minutes afterward, booing the boxers.

Tupac took in the fight with Marion "Suge" (short for his childhood nickname "Sugar Bear") Knight, co-founder and owner of Death Row Records, Tupac's recording label; they sat in seats reserved for them in the front row, some of the best seats in the house. The song that played over the public address system during Tyson's entry into the ring was written by Tupac.

After the fight, Tupac and Suge, along with members of their entourage, were making their way through the casino toward the entrance of the hotel when they got into a scuffle with a then-unidentified black man, whom police would later learn was 22-year-old Orlando Anderson of Compton, California. This fight-outside-the-fight became enormously significant in light of the events that followed.

After security guards broke up the altercation, Tupac, Suge, and their crew headed for the valet area, got into about a dozen high-priced luxury cars, and left the MGM Grand in a caravan headed for the Luxor Hotel, a block south across the Las Vegas Strip. Tupac was staying with his girlfriend Kidada Jones, Quincy Jones' daughter, in one of the rooms Suge Knight had booked at Luxor for the weekend.

Tupac changed his clothes from a tan silk shirt and blue jeans to a black-and-white basketball tank top, bluish-green baggy sweat pants, and black-and-white leather sports shoes. He was wearing a large round gold medallion on a chain around his neck. It wasn't the medallion Suge gave him when he bailed Tupac out of jail a year earlier—the one with the diamond-studded Death Row insignia, a hooded prisoner strapped into an electric chair. The medallion Tupac wore to the fight was the size of a paperweight—and probably just as heavy—picturing a haloed and winged black man wrestling a serpent with one hand and holding a gun in the other.

Tupac didn't pack a weapon that night. He also didn't wear a flak (or bullet-resistant) jacket. Friends say Tupac usually wore a Kevlar vest for fear of being shot. But not that night. He always felt safe when he visited Las Vegas. After all, it was a party town and he was going there to "kick it" and watch his buddy Iron Mike kick butt. Besides, a flak jacket would be too hot in the desert heat, he told Kidada when she packed his clothes earlier that day.

Waiting for their cars in Luxor's valet area, Tupac and

his friends were videotaped on a tourist's camcorder smiling and chatting casually with a couple of women.

When the cars were delivered a few minutes later, the group piled in again and drove to Suge Knight's Las Vegas residence in the southeastern valley, on Monte Rosa Avenue in the Paradise Valley Township. The Las Vegas subdivision boasts some of the oldest estates in Las Vegas Valley and is home to many of the wealthiest and most powerful Las Vegans.

Las Vegas Metropolitan Police Department's Sergeant Kevin Manning, who led the homicide investigation, said the group went to Suge's house to relax before attending a benefit party at a Las Vegas nightspot, located at 1700 East Flamingo Road, known as Club 662. After his fight with Seldon, Tyson was scheduled to appear at Club 662, which Suge ran and, some say, held a financial interest in.

At about 10 p.m., after others in the group had changed their clothes and had a few drinks, the entourage left Suge's house and headed back to the action. Tupac rode shotgun with Suge driving the car Death Row had rented for him: a 1996 black 750 BMW sedan, with dark-tinted windows, chrome wheels, leather upholstery, and a sunroof. The music was cranked up on the car stereo and they were in a partying mood as the caravan of luxury cars—a Lexus, a BMW wagon, a Miata, and a Mercedes Benz—carrying friends and bodyguards followed them.

They cruised the three-mile-long Las Vegas Boulevard, commonly referred to as the Strip, which was jammed with the kind of stop-and-go traffic that is the norm for a Saturday fight night. The sunroof of the BMW was open and the windows rolled down. Suge and Tupac were hollering above the hip-hop blaring from the car's speakers. Tupac and his crew, easily recognized, were turning heads on the Strip. A photographer shot a frame of Tupac and Suge sitting in the car. The photo would later garner between $800 and $5,000 each time it was sold for publication in entertainment and business magazines or to air on TV tabloid and news shows. It was the last photo taken of Tupac alive.

At 11:05 p.m., Suge Knight was stopped on Las Vegas Boulevard by Metro patrol cops for playing the car stereo too loudly and for not having license plates displayed on the BMW. A few minutes later, the officers let Suge go without ticketing him. Tupac and Suge laughed about it as they rounded the corner onto Flamingo Road, heading past Bally's toward Club 662 just two miles away.

They never made it.

Most of Tupac's bodyguards, including former Orange County Sheriff's Department reserve deputy Frank Alexander, and their associates decided not to arm themselves before going to Club 662. They felt the same as Tupac; they were going to a party in a town far removed—or so they thought—from the gang street violence associated with Los Angeles. They probably could have slipped their guns into the MGM Grand Garden that night if they'd wanted to. According to John Husk, executive director of the MGM's arena operations, "There were no metal detectors used at the Mike Tyson fight on September 7."

Las Vegas Metropolitan Police were out in droves and private security was heavy at the Grand Garden during the fight. Sergeant Ron Swift, with Metro's Special Events Section, said officers were assigned inside the casino near the boxing arena to strengthen the hotel's own security.

"On property, we had some officers augmenting hotel security at the event itself," Swift said. "We do it at every major fight, as well as at concerts, rodeos, and parades."

The arena was not the only place cops were assigned to provide a show of force. Special-events officers, working overtime, were stationed at the gate to Suge's neighborhood, which Metro, because of a county ordinance, does not patrol. The homeowners associations of many gated communities in the Las Vegas Valley hire private security officers to patrol inside their walls. Metro police were also contracted to be present at Club 662 after the fight. Overtime for the off-duty Metro police officers was billed to Death Row Records.

"[Death Row] asked us to do it," Sergeant Swift said. "My only concern at the time was traffic and public safety. If a company comes in and asks for extra security, we provide it. Death Row requested it formally from Metro."

One officer claimed that Death Row asked that only African-American cops be assigned to work both Club 662 and Suge's house. "The request was made for only black police officers," the source said.

But Swift couldn't confirm it. "I've never heard that Knight requested black officers. The request may have come in, but I didn't hear about it." A black sergeant, along with six to eight other black officers, were assigned to the party at Suge Knight's house following the fight, the source revealed.

Tupac felt safe as he rode toward Club 662 in the BMW— Suge was driving, friends and bodyguards were nearby, and Metro cops were stationed at the house and the club. In fact, the party at Club 662 was sponsored by Metro Police officer Patrick Barry, a retired professional boxer, to raise money for Barry's Boxing Gym on Vanessa Drive in the southwest area of the Las Vegas Valley. Tupac, Run DMC, and Danny Boy were scheduled to perform at the charity event, intended, ironically, to raise money to keep children away from violence. Club 662's marquee advertised the event as "Barry's Boxing Benefit," produced by SKP (Suge Knight Productions). A line started forming outside the club at 5:30 p.m.; hundreds of people paid $75 each to get in.

Barry's Boxing Benefit, organized by Las Vegas attorney George Kelesis, who once represented Suge, would also help Tupac stay out of prison by fulfilling a court order and condition of probation in one of his criminal cases, in which he was ordered to perform community service in lieu of jail time.

The convoy was headed east on Flamingo Road when it stopped for a red light at Koval Lane, a busy intersection only a half mile from the Strip across from the Maxim Hotel. One associate pulled up a car-length ahead to the right. Another car stopped directly behind them; in it were rapper Yafeu Fula and two associates, one a bodyguard and the other a rapper. Another car was in front of the BMW at the stoplight. The sidewalk and street were heavy with pedestrians.

The BMW was boxed in.

Four young black women, sitting at the stoplight in a Chrysler sedan next to the BMW, turned, smiled at Suge and Tupac, and caught their attention.

A moment later, a late-model Cadillac with three to four black men inside pulled up directly to the right of the BMW, skidding to a stop. A gunman sitting in the back seat stuck a weapon out of the left-rear window of the light-colored Caddy, in full view of the entourage. The gunman tracked Tupac from inside the Cadillac.

Suge and Tupac saw the Caddy, but they had no time to react. Suddenly, the sounds of the night were shattered by the pop pop pop of a killer inside the Cadillac emptying a magazine clip from a high-powered semiautomatic handgun. At least 13 rounds were sprayed (that's how many bullet holes and casings investigators counted) into the passenger side of the BMW. Five bullets pierced the passenger door; some shattered the windows.

Startled, Tupac tried frantically to scramble into the back seat through the well between the front seats. In doing so, he exposed his middle and lower torso to the gunfire and took a round in the hip. Suge grabbed Tupac, pulled him down, and covered him. He yelled, "Get down!" That's when Suge was hit with a fragment in the back of his neck.

Tupac was plugged with bullets at close range. Three rounds pierced his body. One bullet lodged in his chest, entering under his right arm. Another went through his hip, slicing through his lower abdomen, and ended up floating around in his pelvis. Yet another bullet hit his left hand, shattering the bone of his index finger and knocking off a large chunk of gold from a ring he was wearing on another finger. The gunfire nailed Tupac to the leather bucket seat. Glass and blood were everywhere.

Suge was grazed in the neck from the flying shrapnel and glass fragments. A small fragment lodged in the back of his skull at the base of his neck. Bullets also blew out two of the BMW's tires.

The gunfire ended as quickly as it began. The shooting of Tupac Shakur, executed in cold blood, was over in a matter of seconds.

"You hit?" Suge asked Tupac.

"I'm hit," Tupac answered.

Some reports and Metro Police sources say members of the entourage immediately returned fire. Although no other casings were found, police said revolvers may have been used, which leave no telltale shells behind.

Sergeant Manning admitted, "We did hear reports that gunfire was returned, but we were unable to validate it. There was no evidence."

Two Metro Police bicycle patrol officers were on a call concerning a stolen vehicle in the parking garage at the Maxim when they heard the first shots fired at 11:17 p.m. They immediately hopped on their mountain bikes and pedaled toward the street, where they heard more gunfire. They saw the black BMW trying to make a getaway from the gunman. The Cadillac, according to witnesses, floored it and fled. The driver made a right turn onto Koval Lane and vanished. It happened so fast that by the time the bicycle cops arrived seconds later, there was no trace of the Cadillac.

Drivers who witnessed the shooting stopped and stared, dumbfounded. Other cars cut around them, driving over the crime scene and the spent bullets. Horrified pedestrians milled about the sidewalks.

At least six cars behind Tupac tried chasing the Cadillac as it sped south on Koval Lane, away from the scene. The rest stayed with Tupac and Suge.

Suge panicked. He knew he had to find a doctor for Tupac, and quickly. Tupac looked like he was dying, bleeding to death. Suge was splattered with both Tupac's and his own blood. Tupac's breathing was labored and shallow. But his eyes were open wide and he was alert.

Suge had a flip Motorola cellular telephone with him, resting on the car's console, but he didn't use it to call 911 for help. With adrenaline pumping and Tupac bleeding heavily as he sat slumped in the front seat, Suge somehow managed to make a U-turn in the heavy traffic, even though his car now had two flat tires.

"[The bike cops] saw about ten cars pull U-turns and head west on Flamingo at a high rate of speed," Sergeant Greg McCurdy told the *Las Vegas Sun*. Not all the cars stayed with Suge, though, once they saw they were being followed by the cops. Three followed him all the way to the Strip.

Both bicycle cops were at the rear of the caravan, pedaling fast behind them, tailing Suge's BMW, which was now headed toward the crowded Strip. Why one officer didn't follow Suge while the other stayed at the shooting scene is surprising. The officers said it was because they didn't know what had gone down at that point. They'd heard shots being fired—no question about that—but they made a split-second decision not to stay and secure the scene. They felt it was more important to follow Suge and his entourage. It would prove to be the first of several questionable decisions made early on in the investigation.

The scene of the shooting wasn't secured for maybe 20 minutes while cars and pedestrians trampled over the evidence. No one will ever know how many potential witnesses left that scene when no officers were there to hold them.

As Suge made the U-turn, he said to Tupac, "You need a hospital. I'm gonna get you to a hospital right now."

"*I* need a hospital?" Tupac replied. "*You* the one shot in the head. Don't you think you need a hospital?" He started moaning, but managed to utter, "Gotta keep your eyes open."

With three cars full of associates still following close behind him, Suge, for some reason, headed back to the Strip. Bike officer Paul Ehler continued pedaling as he radioed for backup and medical assistance. Fifty yards up Flamingo, Suge got snarled in traffic. He frantically weaved the BMW in and out of the left-turn lane and over the median, then floored it.

Suge made it to the Strip, hitting a red light. Instead of stopping, though, he screeched through the intersection. His rims caught the center divider as he turned left onto the boulevard, giving the car its third flat tire. Suge then straightened out the steering wheel and drove south down Las Vegas Boulevard. He weaved in and out of the busy traffic for a quarter of a mile, running another red light at Harmon Avenue. There, exactly a mile from the shooting scene, Suge Knight's BMW got caught up on the median, then lunged back onto the street, and came to a grinding halt in the middle of the busy Strip. It now had four flat tires.

That's when the Strip got really crazy.

Sirens from patrol cruisers, ambulances, a fire department rescue unit, and the highway patrol screamed as every available unit converged on the scene.

Cops were yelling at everyone in Tupacs's entourage, ordering them to get out of their cars and "get their faces on the ground," to lie flat on their stomachs with their hands behind their heads. The police held some of the entourage at gunpoint. Even Suge Knight, bleeding from his head wound, was ordered to lie face down on the pavement until the police figured out what was going on.

Blood was everywhere. The BMW's leather seats were soaked with it and Tupac's cotton shirt was solid crimson.

By the time the paramedics arrived a few minutes later, the cops had things under control. They let the members of Tupac's entourage get up off the street one by one and sit on the curb of the Strip sidewalk while they waited for general-assignment and homicide detectives to arrive.

Tupac was conscious but short of breath as the emergency response teams prepared to rush him and Suge to University Medical Center, Las Vegas' county hospital, a few miles away. Tupac was first to go. He was still alert, with his eyes open, watching what was going on. He was lifted onto a gurney and put into the ambulance. Just as paramedics were closing the back doors to the ambulance, witnesses heard Tupac say quietly, "I'm dyin', man."

Tupac Shakur would succumb to his wounds six days later.

2

THE AFTERMATH

Yafeu Fula was a rapper in the group Outlaw Immortalz, which backed up and toured with Tupac. He was in the car directly behind Suge's rented BMW when the shooting occurred and he stayed with the BMW as it careened down Flamingo Avenue and the Strip. Fula was questioned by detectives at the scene, then rode to University Medical Center where Tupac was being treated.

While on his way to the hospital, Yafeu Fula used a cell phone to call his mother, Yaasmyn, and tell her what had happened. He said, "Call Afeni and tell her Tupac's been shot."

Yaasmyn Fula called her good friend Afeni Shakur and broke the news that Tupac had been gunned down and it was bad. By the time Afeni Shakur was contacted by Yaasmyn, it was morning in Stone Mountain, Georgia, about 20 miles northeast of Atlanta, where Afeni lived in a home Tupac had purchased for her through his record company. Afeni notified other family members and then, accompanied by Tupac's half-sister Sekyiwa Shakur and cousin Deena, caught the earliest flight available to Las Vegas.

They arrived in the afternoon and checked into Room 1039 at the Golden Nugget Hotel on Fremont Street in downtown Las Vegas. Then they left for University Medical Center, about five miles away on West Charleston. Thus the official death watch began. For the next six days, Tupac's family, friends, and fans kept a twenty-four-hour vigil at the hospital.

The night before, when Tupac and Suge arrived at the hospital in the ambulances, Suge was admitted and placed in a regular hospital room. Tupac was taken to the trauma center's intensive-care unit, where a medical team prepped him for emergency surgery.

A few hours later, hospital spokesman Dale Pugh walked outside and told the big crowd of waiting reporters, "He's had a right lung removed, he's back in his room, and he remains in critical condition. He has been conscious. He is under a lot of medication, so he's pretty sedated at this time. He's severely injured. Suffering multiple gunshot wounds is obviously a terrible insult to the human body, so he's requiring intensive care, and he is receiving that right now."

After the surgery, Tupac was placed on a ventilator and respirator, and the next day, still on life-support machines, was put into a drug-induced coma. The only people allowed to visit him that first day, other than family members, were Suge, Mike Tyson, M.C. Hammer, actress Jasmine Guy, Kidada Jones, the Rev. Jesse Jackson, and a local minister, the Rev. Willie Davis. Tyson stood up reporters at a press conference that Sunday after the fight, but he made it to Tupac's bedside.

That morning, Jesse Jackson, accompanied by Rev. James Rogers, president of the local office of the National Association for the Advancement of Colored People, Baptist minister Willie Davis, and NAACP assistant to the president, Rev. Chester Richardson, went to the Second Baptist Church in West Las Vegas. There, Rev. Jackson gave a sermon about Tupac.

"Before you condemn Tupac for calling women bitches

and ho's in his music," Jackson told the parishioners, "you need to understand and know about the background of this man and where he came from. He was raised by a woman who was on crack. He didn't have a real mama. Don't condemn him for talking about his mama and for talking about women." Jackson asked churchgoers to pray for Tupac's recovery. Children and teenagers in the congregation cried as he spoke about the rapper.

After stopping at five churches in West Las Vegas, which is known as the Westside and is the largest African-American community in Las Vegas, Reverend Jackson, who first met Tupac when he was 12, stopped at the hospital to visit him. Reverend Davis drove with Jackson to the hospital's trauma unit, where Jackson stood with Davis and prayed at Tupac's bedside for about 15 minutes.

Outside, plainclothes gang-unit detectives assigned to the hospital kept a watchful eye on the streets surrounding University Medical Center.

M.C. Hammer drove up in his dark-green Hummer and parked on the street in front of the hospital's trauma unit. Unaccompanied, he walked silently past reporters with his head down, ignoring their questions.

That Sunday, T-shirts with Tupac's photo were already being sold on a corner at D Street and Jackson Avenue in the heart of the Westside.

Homicide detectives and crime-scene analysts finished their work at the scene as the sun was rising that Sunday morning, then returned to their offices to work on their reports. Kevin Manning wrote a one-page press release and faxed it to the local media:

LAS VEGAS METROPOLITAN POLICE DEPARTMENT
MEDIA RELEASE

September 8, 1996
Event #: 960908-2063

SGT. KEVIN MANNING
HOMICIDE SECTION
PHONE: 229-3521

September 8, 1996: At approximately 11:15 p.m., LVMPD patrol officers were at the Maxim Hotel on an unrelated call when they heard several shots being fired from Flamingo Road and Koval Lane. The officers looked to the area of the shots from the Maxim parking garage. They saw several vehicles and numerous people in the street. Several of the vehicles made a U-turn from eastbound Flamingo to westbound Flamingo, leaving the area at a high rate of speed.

The vehicles were stopped at the intersection of Las Vegas Blvd. and Harmon. Bike patrol officers were first on the scene and discovered two men suffering from gunshot wounds. Medical assistance was requested and the two victims were transported to UMC-Trauma.

The victims have been identified as Tupac Shakur, 25, and Marion Knight, 31. Shakur was the passenger in the vehicle and received several gunshot wounds. He was still in surgery and the injuries were considered serious. Knight received a minor wound to the head and was expected to be treated and released.

The investigation so far has determined that the Shakur and Knight group had attended the Tyson fight and were headed for a local nightclub. The group consisted of approximately 10 vehicles that were traveling in a loose convoy. As the vehicles approached the intersection of Flamingo and Koval, a late '90s, white, 4-door Cadillac containing four people pulled up beside the Shakur/Knight vehicle and one of the people in the Cadillac started shooting into the Shakur/ Knight vehicle. The suspect vehicle then fled south on Koval.

Anyone with information in regards to this incident is urged to call Secret Witness at 385-5555 or Metro Homicide at 229-3521.

Two detectives, Brent Becker and Mike Franks, waited outside Suge Knight's hospital room early Sunday morning to interview him about what he saw. Suge claimed to be too busy with visitors passing through his room to talk to police. Suge instructed a nurse to ask the detectives to come back later. But at 11 o'clock Sunday morning, Suge was released— before the detectives returned to the hospital to take his statement. Suge went home to his Las Vegas estate without giving a witness statement to the police.

Two days later, on Tuesday, Suge Knight's three attorneys, David Chesnoff and Steve Steiner in Las Vegas and David Kenner from Los Angeles, made arrangements with detectives to meet at homicide headquarters on West Charleston Boulevard about four miles from the hospital. All three are defense attorneys.

Sergeant Manning said detectives had "many conversations with the attorneys" in setting up the meeting. The lawyers told the investigators that Suge was still recovering from his shrapnel wound. But their biggest fear, attorneys told detectives, was that Suge would be inundated by the press before and after the meeting. To guard against this, neither the time nor the location of the meeting was released to the media beforehand.

Sergeant Manning and detectives Franks and Becker waited three hours on Tuesday, September 10, but the foursome never showed. The investigators grew impatient and went home for the night. One of Suge's attorneys later told the detectives that they did go to homicide headquarters that evening, but not until after 6 p.m., when no one was there.

The next day, Wednesday, September 11, four days after the shooting, Suge Knight and his attorneys again made arrangements and did finally meet with police at homicide headquarters. Detectives interviewed Suge for less than an hour (one detective said it was about 30 minutes, another said 45 minutes) in an interview room off the lobby of the single-story office complex.

Suge offered little, if any, new information. He told them he "heard something, but saw nothing."

"We were hoping he would tell us who shot him," Sergeant Manning said. "He didn't give us anything beneficial. Nothing he said helped us."

Manning said the only real evidence investigators had was "the number of bullet holes in the passenger door of the BMW."

Manning issued a press release the day after homicide's interview with Suge Knight, dated September 12, 1996.

LATEST INFORMATION REGARDING THE
LESANE P. CROOKS (A K A TUPAC SHAKUR)
AND MARION H. KNIGHT (A K A SUGE)
SHOOTING UPDATE

On the evening of 9/11/96, the attorneys for Marion "Suge" Knight made arrangements for Knight to be interviewed by LVMPD homicide investigators.

Knight made himself available for the interview, but was unable to give the investigators any information that would help in determining a motive, nor was he able to help identify possible suspects.

The investigation is at the same juncture. Investigators are hopeful someone will be able to provide information [of] substance.

A $1,000 reward is available for information leading to the arrest and conviction of the suspects. Anyone with information is urged to contact Secret Witness at (702) 385-5555 or LVMPD homicide at 229-3521.

Meanwhile, Tupac remained in a coma. A doctor treating him said only that he had a fifty-fifty chance of survival. However, Dr. John Fildes, medical director of the University Medical Center's trauma unit, elaborated, telling a reporter that the gunshot wounds Tupac suffered usually proved fatal, but that Tupac had passed a critical phase.

"Overall, of all comers with a gunshot wound in the chest that passes through the blood vessels connecting the heart and lungs, only one in five survive," Fildes said. "The majority die in the first twenty-four to forty-eight hours from shock and bleeding during the treatment and surgery phase."

For victims who survive the first twenty-four hours, he said, "the chances of survival would be more than one in five." He said patients with wounds similar to Tupac's also "die during the second major risk period, after five or seven days, when difficulties in oxygenation or the presence of infections or other complications arise." Fildes emphasized that he wasn't treating Shakur, but simply commenting on the chances of survival for someone suffering such injuries.

Tupac underwent two surgeries to stop the internal bleeding. The second was to remove his right lung, a measure doctors said was the only way to stop the bleeding. Still, the bleeding didn't stop and his doctors were stumped. A third surgery was scheduled, but Tupac Shakur died before it could be done.

It was Friday the 13th.

• • •

Danny Boy, a teenage rapper and rhythm and blues singer with the Death Row label who was said to be Suge's next hit-maker and Tupac's protege, broke down and crumbled to the sidewalk outside University Medical Center upon hearing the news of Tupac's death. Danny Boy was the only man at the hospital that day who openly wept for Tupac.

Afeni Shakur made the decision not to resuscitate her son, she later told ABC's "Prime Time Live." "I really felt it was important for Tupac, who fought so hard, to have a free spirit. I felt it was important for his spirit to be allowed to be free. So I rejoiced with him, with the release of his spirit. I rejoiced then and I rejoice now, when I'm not crying."

More and more of Tupac's friends filed into the trauma unit after news of his death spread. A crowd of roughly 75 mourners gathered outside the hospital. A nurse said evening-shift employees scheduled to work that night called in sick because they were afraid to walk through the crowd. Dozens of police surrounded the area, but there were no problems.

A black Lexus drove up to the hospital, pulling over in a no-parking zone in front of the trauma center. Danny Boy cried as he embraced one of the men who got out of the car.

It was Suge Knight.

Suge—six-foot-four and weighing about 315 pounds—was wearing a crisp white T-shirt, black jeans, and brand new white leather sports shoes. He was smoking a cigar. He opened the front passenger door and got out of the car. Holding the cigar in his right hand, he slowly sauntered from the curbside, strolling past Metro gang cops, fans, and a few reporters. After hugging Danny Boy, he walked through the glass doors to the trauma center's lobby.

Few people appeared to recognize Suge. They just stood quietly by and watched. Only one photographer took a photo as Suge approached the hospital to pay his respects to Tupac's mother. Suge looked right through the photographer with a blank stare, and kept walking. His face was emotionless.

Suge had the air of the linebacker and bodyguard he used to be as he somberly walked by. He appeared unconcerned for his own safety, despite rumors circulating that there were three contracts on his head and that he, not Tupac, had been the intended target of the shooters.

What no one knew then—except the cops—was that Suge had gone that day to register as a felon in the state of Nevada. As a convicted felon, he was required to tell his parole officer he was leaving California and, within 48 hours of arriving in Nevada, he was mandated by law to register with Metro. He did that on the day Tupac succumbed to his wounds.

Six days after Tupac was gunned down, Suge had his mug shot taken, was fingerprinted, and put in the state's convicted-felon registry.

Once inside the hospital lobby, Suge comforted Afeni Shakur and told her not to worry, that he and Death Row Records would take care of her financially. He told her that he and Tupac had made a promise to each other: the family of whoever died first would be taken care of by the other.

Tupac's mother told Suge that if there was to be a memorial service, she wanted everyone to wear white, not black. Suge, in a video about Tupac's life titled *Thug Immortal*, said Afeni told him, "'Tupac has gone to a better place. He's free now. Nobody can do nothing to him.'"

"I sat back and I thought, 'Yeah, can't nobody arrest him,'" Suge remembered. "'Can't nobody try to put him down. Can't nobody fire shots at him. Can't nobody hurt him no more.' He's in heaven, in a better place."

After learning that Tupac's body had already been removed from the hospital, Suge and the men he came with walked out of the hospital, quietly got into the Lexus, and drove away. Gang cops appeared relieved.

Word began to circulate that the coroner had used the back entrance to remove Tupac's body, taking him in a van from the hospital to the coroner's office around the corner. Danny Boy walked to the front of the hospital to the driveway used by ambulances, sat down on a curb with a friend, and sobbed again. A crew member put his arm around him and comforted him. They stayed there for about 15 minutes.

Some of the fans who'd been keeping the hospital vigil left and went to the coroner's office, where Tupac's autopsy would be performed.

"We had them at our back doors. We had them driving by. We had them calling. It got ridiculous," said Ron Flud, who has been the Clark County Coroner for 13 years and was a cop with the North Las Vegas Police Department before that. "We had local ministers show up and say, 'Suge wanted us here.' First of all, as far as coming into the office, only the next of kin has any kind of control over the body. And the only reason you let them in is to identify the body. Tupac had already been identified [by his mother]. We're dealing with evidence and we're very protective as to who is going to be around. Nobody goes into the autopsy except who we control. There were requests to be there from all kinds of people—medical personnel, cops, firefighters. We said, 'Why?'"

Reporters and photographers waited outside the trauma unit for more than two hours for the hospital spokesman, Dale Pugh, to issue an official statement confirming that Tupac had died. One was Kevin Powell, a freelance rap journalist on assignment for *Rolling Stone* magazine who'd befriended Tupac after interviewing him many times over several years. Powell looked sad as he stood by, notebook at his side, silently watching the group of mourners. Powell, a cast member on the MTV series "Real World" in 1992 and host-writer for MTV's documentary "Straight From The Hood," described Tupac as his friend and said he didn't think Tupac was going to die. Powell called him tough, especially after surviving a shooting two years earlier. The Tupac he knew was a fighter.

Reporters continued to wait, as they're accustomed to doing at crime scenes, hospitals, and courtrooms. Finally, they were told that Dale Pugh wouldn't be coming out after all. Apparently, he felt he might be putting himself in danger by walking outside of his hospital to talk to the media.

"I never had a plan to come down and talk to the news media," Pugh said afterwards. "Our decision was made. We knew how we were going to handle it if [Tupac] passed away. Our efforts were to *call* everyone in the press. We'd had so many telephone calls concerning it. The media from around the world was calling, besides calls from fans. The hospital was deluged with calls about Tupac.

"Our main thing was to inform the local media that he had died and then return telephone calls. That's how we handled it because of the volume. I don't think we've ever in the history of this hospital held a press conference, nor will we probably ever do that. That's not the way we choose to handle that kind of thing."

Many hospitals, especially in California, hold press conferences for high-profile people or events. Not in Las Vegas.

"To have celebrities here is not unusual," Pugh said. "We've had [lots of them]. I remember one out-of-state politician who was here. Bob Stupak [a flamboyant casino mogul who was nearly killed in a motorcycle accident in 1995] was here—that's well known. Brent Thurman, the National Finals Rodeo rider who died, was here. In none of those instances did we hold any sort of press conference. We did individual news interviews."

As it turned out, it was a peaceful and somber crowd—mostly mourners—who stood outside the hospital that afternoon and into the evening. No one appeared to be threatening. Cars drove slowly by the hospital as word of Tupac Shakur's death spread on TV, radio, and the Internet. Some passengers in the cars threw gang hand signs at the people standing outside, but no one reacted. Tupac's lyrics blared from some of their car stereos.

Tupac's futile six-day battle to survive marked the end of a lifetime raked with emotional and physical struggles, first on the streets and later on the entertainment scene.

His death rocked the gangsta rap world to its core. Black leaders called for peace among the rappers, and politicians (including Vice President Al Gore's wife, Tipper, on a visit to Las Vegas) denounced the violence in gangsta-rap lyrics.

But that didn't quell the gunfire. The week after Tupac Shakur was shot, bullets riddled the gang-infested streets of Los Angeles as drive-by shootings broke out at a record pace. Southern California police noted 12 retaliation shootings— three deadly—the following week. Two months later, the lone witness to the shooting, Yafeu Fula, was murdered in New Jersey. Six months later, East Coast superstar rapper Biggie Smalls, under contract to Death Row Records' rival label, Bad Boy Entertainment, was shot to death in a drive-by shooting, similar to the one that claimed Tupac, in Los Angeles.

Meanwhile, Death Row Records, Tupac's label, started to unravel. Suge Knight, CEO of Death Row, jailed two months after the shooting for a parole violation, was sentenced to nine years in prison for his role in the fight at the MGM Grand just hours before Tupac was shot. The FBI and IRS were looking into Death Row's books and associations. Also in the aftermath, the slayings of the two hottest hip-hop stars stirred criticism of the rap world and made record companies uneasy, but the murders didn't hurt sales or deter fans; it was just the opposite. Both Tupac's and Biggie's final albums went to number one on *Billboard Magazine's* record charts. Tupac's last album *Makaveli* and Biggie Smalls' album *Life After Death...'Til Death Do Us Part*, both released posthumously, broke all-time sales records, generating talk that the two rap superstars were worth more dead than alive.

All the while, Las Vegas Metropolitan Police continued to investigate Tupac Shakur's murder and critics, including Tupac's mother, her attorney, and witnesses griped about Metro's handling of the case from the first moments following the shooting.

3

THE SCUFFLE

The Mike Tyson-Bruce Seldon match was supposed to begin at 8 o'clock sharp that Saturday night, September 7, but it started about 15 minutes late. Tyson knocked out Seldon in the first round in less than two minutes.

Tupac Shakur, Suge Knight, and their entourage walked out of the fight venue, the MGM Grand Garden, and into the casino. Tupac was spotted leaving the arena by freelance video cameraman Cornell Wade, who worked for a Las Vegas-based video-services company that films celebrities for television shows. That night Wade was contracted by Black Entertainment Television (BET). The BET reporter he was with had trouble getting out of the crowded arena, and as the cameraman stood outside the exit waiting for her, he saw Tupac walking out of the Garden and through the turnstiles.

Wade was in the middle of interviewing Louis Gossett Jr. when he spotted Tupac. Unlike Gossett, Tupac wasn't one of the celebrities Wade was assigned to film, but he thought, "What the heck. I'll [film] him anyway." He wrapped up his interview with Gossett and walked a few steps toward Tupac. He said, "I'm with Black Entertainment Television. Can I ask you about the fight?"

"Sure. No problem, man. Go ahead," Tupac replied as

Suge Knight stood quietly behind him.

Wade put a mike in front of him and switched on the camera. "What'd you think of tonight's match?"

Tupac looked straight into the camera lens and said, "Did y'all see that? Fifty punches. I counted. Fifty punches. I knew he was gonna take him out. We bad like that—come outta prison and now we runnin' shit."

It was the last interview of Tupac's life.

Later, when the reporter learned that Tupac had been at the Tyson fight and had been shot afterward, she commented to Wade, "I wish we would have gotten video of him."

"I did," the cameraman said. "I got it." He handed the tape over to BET, even though he probably could have sold it to the TV tabloids. The short interview aired on a number of local and national TV news programs for several days following the shooting.

At 8:45 p.m., as Tupac, Suge, and their friends were walking through the casino on their way to pick up their cars at valet parking, they ran into Orlando Tive Anderson, from Compton, California, and a fight ensued.

Exactly what precipitated the fight is unknown, but there were rumors that Anderson, also known as "Little Lando" and "Land," tried to grab a large gold medallion with the Death Row Records insignia from the neck of one of Tupac's friends. Tupac and the group, in turn, reportedly jumped Anderson. There were also reports that Tupac and Orlando had exchanged heated words earlier in the evening inside the Grand Garden waiting for the bout to begin and that they'd carried the beef outside. Anderson and his friends were said to be sitting in the front-row seats reserved for Tupac and Suge when the entourage walked in to watch the fight. Those rumors have not been substantiated.

Hotel security guards quickly converged on the altercation with Anderson and broke it up.

After the scuffle, Tupac and his crew hurriedly left the scene while an unnamed MGM Grand security guard called in Metro Police, already on premises to work the fight. The officers talked to the security guard and the victim, whose identity they didn't establish. The Metro cops offered to take the man to the MGM Grand's security office in the basement to fill out a police incident report and sign a complaint, but the man declined. He told them he was okay and that he didn't want to press charges. Because he refused, and appeared to be uninjured except for bruises, the officers didn't even write down his name before letting him walk away.

In the state of Nevada, if a victim of a crime declines to file a report, then police let the victim go. That's the law.

"No victim, no crime," explained Metro Lieutenant Wayne Petersen, who heads the homicide unit, defending security's failure to identify the victim. "In a misdemeanor battery like this one, if the victim chooses not to fill out a crime report, we can't force him to. It's not unusual at all. It happens all the time. And we certainly aren't going to generate more work for ourselves and take a report if the victim is not willing to cooperate. In court, to prosecute, you have to have the victim's testimony."

The scuffle was captured on an MGM security videotape. The murky recording shows seven to eight men—Tupac, Suge, their paid bodyguards, and other members of the entourage—throwing the then-unidentified black man to the casino floor, then beating and stomping him.

"They kicked the holy shit out of him," said a police source who viewed the entire unedited version of the surveillance videotape. "They beat him up pretty bad."

But because the original videotape was grainy and indistinct, it was hard to tell exactly what was going on, according to homicide Detective Brent Becker. "It's like a pile of people," he said.

On September 11, Metro Police issued a third news release. It said:

"The LVMPD homicide investigators have viewed a surveillance tape provided by the MGM Grand. The tape depicts an altercation between Tupac Shakur, some of his associates, and an unknown person. The altercation was broken up immediately by security. Shakur and his people left the area. The unknown person was then interviewed by MGM security and LVMPD patrol officers.

"The unknown person was asked if he wished to file a report, but he declined. It does not appear that the person or the patrol officers knew that Shakur was the other person in the altercation. The unknown person was still with security and patrol officers when Shakur and his associates left the building.

"Investigators have no reason, at this time, to believe that the altercation has any connection to the shooting.

"The videotape will not be released since it appears to have no evidentiary value to the shooting incident."

Why didn't the police and security officers detain Tupac Shakur and members of his entourage for questioning after the attack on Orlando Anderson? Though the official statement denies it, surely those first to the scene knew that Tupac was involved. Was it Suge's and Tupac's celebrity status that allowed them to walk away from an obvious crime? Was it Suge's business connection to Metro? After all, off-duty Metro officers at that very minute were being paid time and a half by Death Row to patrol Suge's house and club. Later, just 15 minutes before the shooting, Suge would again be treated preferentially when he was stopped, but not cited, for failure to display a license plate on his car and for playing his music too loudly. Did the polite police behavior stem from a fear of offending a celebrity? Police say no.

Contrary to the claim in the news release that the videotape would not be released, it was subsequently relinquished by Metro. While continuing to deny that the beating was related to Tupac's homicide, Metro released the tape to Fox's "America's Most Wanted" television program. Later it was subpoenaed by the Los Angeles Superior Court for Suge Knight's parole-violation proceedings, where it became public record.

Another surveillance tape shows an agitated Tupac and his friends storming through the casino. Suge can be seen running behind Tupac, trying to catch up, with members of their entourage following behind them. Tupac slammed his hand against an MGM glass entrance door as he huffily left the casino for the valet area.

After the existence of the surveillance tapes became widely known to the media, Sergeant Manning dismissed the incident, saying, "It appears to be just an individual who was walking through the MGM and got into an argument with Tupac. The man probably didn't know who he was dealing with. He probably didn't know it was Tupac Shakur."

The victim "wasn't dressed like everyone else," an investigator said. "The subject was wearing a ballclub shirt, like a team jersey, and wasn't dressed up like Shakur and his group." In other words, he didn't look like he fit in with Tupac and his flashy West Coast crew, who were wearing expensive clothes and jewelry.

At some point, and privately, the investigators changed their minds. The videotape of the scuffle became evidence. What had been a minor fight-night incident turned into an event of enormous significance in the grand scheme of the investigation.

"Any of those incidents leading up to Tupac's death obviously are of interest from an investigative standpoint," Petersen later said. "[But] we don't have a case. We've got no evidence linking [Orlando Anderson] to this [murder]."

The surveillance videotape was forwarded to the evidence vault for storage several months after the murder.

After the shooting, homicide detectives scrambled to learn the identity of the victim in the MGM scuffle by talking to the officers who responded that night. Only the man's first name, "Orlando," could be recalled. That was enough according to police. How the first name of a young black man could have been enough information for Metro detectives to contact the Compton Police Department is unclear. But Compton police gave Metro Orlando Anderson, who was allegedly tied to the Los Angeles Southside Crips street gang, and quickly dispatched a photo of him, a mug shot from a previous arrest. The photo was shown to the officers and security guards working at the MGM Grand on September 7 to see if they could identify him. They positively ID'd him as the victim of the beating.

Only four days after the shooting, on Wednesday, September 11, Los Angeles-area police raided a Compton house, responding to reports that the men inside had weapons. When police arrived, they found Orlando Anderson and four other alleged Crips members standing in the front yard of the house. Anderson reportedly ran inside, followed closely by police. Upon questioning, he claimed he didn't live there, even though a high school diploma bearing his name hung on a bedroom wall, police said. Inside, police found an AK-47 assault rifle, a .38-caliber revolver, two shotguns, a 9-millimeter M-11 assault pistol, and ammunition. They confiscated the weapons. But because Anderson insisted he didn't live in the house and police had no real evidence to prove otherwise, they let him go.

In the days following, police began focusing on Orlando Anderson as a possible suspect in Tupac's murder. They said they'd received several tips accusing him of being connected to the killing.

An affidavit signed by Compton Police Detective Tim Brennan, dated September 25, 1996, and unsealed in February 1997 in Los Angeles Superior Court, read: "Informants have told police that Southside Crips were responsible for the Las Vegas shooting [of Shakur]. There is also an ongoing feud between Tupac Shakur and the Bloods-related Death Row Records with rapper Biggie Smalls and the East Coast's Bad Boy Entertainment, which employed Southside Crips gang members as security."

Bad Boy Entertainment has denied it hired Crips members.

"We have no knowledge of security being provided by

Crips or other gang members," Bad Boy spokeswoman Maureen Connelly said in a published statement. "Bad Boy Entertainment employs full-time security personnel and they [are] supplemented by off-duty members of the Los Angeles police force."

Edi M.O. Faal, Rodney King's attorney now representing Orlando Anderson, though admitting that Anderson was the man assaulted at the MGM Grand by Tupac and his entourage, has denied that his client had any involvement in Tupac's murder.

Anderson himself has also strongly denied any connection to Tupac's death. But Compton police remained convinced that Tupac's murder was due to a Bloods-Crips feud.

In mid-September 1996, Los Angeles police organized a massive predawn sweep of Bloods and Crips neighborhoods in Lakewood, Long Beach, Compton, and L.A. and scheduled the action to go down two weeks later. The raid was organized after three people were killed in 12 shootings that occurred in the Compton area the week following the Shakur shooting, Compton Police Captain Steven Roller told a reporter. He described the violence as possible retaliation for Tupac's murder. Roller is one of the few officers who has publicly acknowledged the possibility that there were acts of retaliation for Tupac's death.

Los Angeles and Compton police planned to serve a search warrant at Orlando Anderson's house as part of the gang raids, and Metro homicide detectives Brent Becker and Mike Franks were invited to be there so they could question him. They arrived in Los Angeles the day before the raid.

On October 2, approximately 300 L.A.-area police and federal agents, most clad in black masks, helmets, and bulletproof vests, raided 37 homes, including Anderson's. Las Vegas Metro's Detective Becker talked with Anderson outside the house he shared with relatives, while Los Angeles-area police searched inside.

Becker, sitting in his car while Anderson stood nearby, said he talked casually with the young Compton resident about the MGM surveillance tape of the scuffle with Tupac, Suge, and other Death Row Records' associates. Becker said he questioned Anderson only about the scuffle at the MGM Grand the night Tupac was shot, and didn't touch on the homicide that followed it.

Later, in a CNN interview, Anderson accused Metro Police and Becker of telling him he was a suspect in Tupac's murder. "I want to let everybody know—you know what I'm saying?—I didn't do it," Anderson told CNN. "I been thinking that maybe I'm a scapegoat or something."

Anderson's lawyer Faal told CNN, "This young man is almost acting like a prisoner now. He is very careful where he goes. He is very careful when he goes out."

Becker and his supervisors maintain that Anderson was merely asked about the fight that was captured on the surveillance tapes, and that Anderson was reading more into the encounter than was there.

Metro Lieutenant Wayne Petersen defended Becker and strongly denied the allegation. "When (Becker) went to Los Angeles to talk to Anderson, he asked Anderson questions only about the fight at the MGM," Petersen insisted. "He never asked him about the homicide. If he wanted to ask him questions about the homicide, he would have had to read him his Miranda rights." Becker told Petersen that "Anderson asked [him] if he was going to take him back to Las Vegas, and Becker's response was 'Why should I?'"

The Los Angeles police raid of gang houses netted 23 arrests, including Anderson's, on various weapons and drug-possession charges. Also confiscated from one of those arrested was a Death Row pendant. Anderson was held for questioning in connection with a 1994 murder, as well as for questioning by Las Vegas Metro police about the scuffle with Tupac and his entourage. But Compton police said they didn't have enough evidence on the 1994 gang-related murder to hold him, and he was released the next day.

Metro police decided not to charge him with Tupac's murder.

The scuffle at the MGM had serious legal repercussions for Suge Knight.

On October 22, 1996, Suge surrendered to Los Angeles police for violating probation, to which he was sentenced in 1995 after pleading no contest to assaulting two rappers at a Hollywood recording studio. (In 1992, brothers George and Stanley Lynwood, two aspiring rappers, used a telephone at Suge's studio without first asking permission. Suge walked in and caught them. He beat one of them with a gun, then threatened to kill them. Then he forced both men to remove their pants. The Lynwoods filed a police complaint. Suge was convicted on assault charges and sentenced to probation.)

Four days earlier on October 18, a warrant for Suge's arrest had been issued for failing to submit to periodic drug tests, one of the conditions of his probation. He was jailed without bail. In early November, Suge was back in court to answer charges that his involvement in the MGM Grand altercation was another violation of his probation.

The small neighborhood of Compton, a largely African-American suburb in South Central Los Angeles, is where Suge Knight grew up (the youngest of three, with two older sisters) and where, police say, he was affiliated with the Bloods street gang. Suge sports a tattoo that reads "M.O.B." which stands for "Member of the Bloods," or "Money Over Bitches" (one of Knight's known mottos), or just plain "Mob," as in the Mafia. M.O.B. also coincides with the telephone numbers 662, which is the significance of the name of Club 662 in Las Vegas, where Tupac and Suge were headed the night of the shooting.

After Orlando Anderson's October arrest in the gang sweep, several people who were arrested with him reportedly told Compton police that Suge was the intended target.

In an affidavit filed November 5, 1996, with Los Angeles Superior Court Judge J. Stephen Czuleger, probation officer Barry Nodorf recommended that Knight's probation remain revoked, and that the defendant remain locked up pending a formal violation hearing.

Judge Czuleger viewed the MGM security videotape in his courtroom. The tape shows a man identified as Suge Knight pushing down another man and kicking him, probation officer Nodorf said in his seven-page report.

"There are compelling reasons to believe that another probation violation has occurred," the report said.

"This fact, coupled with the defendant's potential threat to the community and the possibility of his being a flight risk, leaves the probation officer with no alternative but to make the recommendation" that the defendant remain in jail, where he would spend four months awaiting the hearing's outcome.

Suge's attorney, David Kenner, denounced the report. "The allegation that Suge Knight beat someone up at the MGM is meritless," Kenner told *The Associated Press*.

Knight is visible on the tape, but his actions are obscured by other people and objects. But according to Nodorf, a hotel security guard identified Knight as one of the aggressors in the scuffle. Suge said he was trying to "break up the rumble."

His assertion, strangely enough, was backed up by Orlando Anderson, who testified in Knight's probation-violation hearing that Suge was the only one who helped him that night. Earlier, however, in another court proceeding, Anderson had identified Suge to the judge as one of those *involved* in the scuffle. When pressed, Anderson couldn't give a reason why he later named Suge as the one who came to his rescue.

Had someone gotten to Anderson? That's what investigators speculated, but wouldn't say for the record. Someone, they surmised privately, was persuasive enough with Anderson to make him do an about-face in his testimony under oath. Suge Knight sat in the defendant's chair with a smile on his face while Anderson testified. The judge was not impressed, however. He sentenced Knight to nine years in state prison.

4

THE INVESTIGATION

As far back as anyone in the Las Vegas Metropolitan Police Department can remember, the Tupac Shakur murder case is the biggest Las Vegas has ever seen. But even though it's the biggest and most highly publicized, the killing of Tupac Shakur may never be solved. Even the lieutenant of the homicide section, Wayne Petersen, doesn't believe the murderer will be captured, nor will the case ever be prosecuted.

It's a case Metro probably wishes never came its way—for more reasons than the obvious, the murder of a famous young man. The handling of the investigation has been criticized from start to finish by participants and observers, who contend that the police haven't done everything they could and should have.

According to authorities, it hasn't been for lack of effort, but for lack of cooperation from just about everyone involved—the witnesses, Tupac's associates, Suge Knight, and even police from other departments and jurisdictions.

Seven homicide teams—made up of a sergeant and two detectives—rotate on an on-call basis at Metro. Each three-man team investigates an average of 25 murders a year. (Tupac's was one of 207 homicides in Las Vegas' Clark County in 1996 and one of 168 investigated by Metro that year.) The night Tupac was shot, the team on call consisted of Sergeant Kevin Manning, Detective Brent Becker, and Detective Mike Franks—all veteran detectives.

Brent Becker worked in the robbery section before he moved to homicide. At the time of Tupac's murder, he'd been working the homicide detail for about two years. His partner, Mike Franks, had been working in homicide for four years at the time of the murder. Before that, Franks worked in the narcotics unit with Sergeant Manning. Manning, early in his police career, was a part of Metro's first street-narcotics unit. He'd also worked in the gang detail. When Tupac was shot, Manning had been a homicide sergeant for a year and half.

The Clark County Sheriff's Department merged with Metro in 1973 and became the Metropolitan Police Department. Franks and Manning were hired by Metro; Becker was with the sheriff's department before the two were combined.

"Brent was one of my trainees [at Metro] when I was a training officer," Manning said. "I worked with Mike in narcotics. We're all friends."

The homicide unit at Metro is a somewhat casual bunch. It's an elite group; working homicide is a sought-after assignment. But Las Vegas detectives don't dress the part. They don't wear white dress shirts, neckties, and black slacks like many of their counterparts in other cities. Here in the desert, they're more likely to be seen wearing golf shirts and Dockers.

Manning, Becker, and Franks were called to the scene at Las Vegas Boulevard and Harmon Avenue about an hour and a half after the shooting. The homicide lieutenant at the time, Larry Spinosa, was out of town; otherwise he would've been there too.

In the days and weeks following the homicide, the team interviewed a couple dozen people who were friends or associates of Tupac, some of whom were part of the entourage, and they talked to "literally thousands of people" about the case, Manning said.

Throughout the investigation, police say, witnesses have uniformly refused to cooperate. The detectives were frustrated from the very beginning, stunned by the number of witnesses who claimed not to have seen the assailants, or anything else for that matter.

"The witness statements were pretty similar: 'I didn't see nothin'. I didn't know nobody. I wasn't even there,'" Lieutenant Wayne Petersen commented, mocking the language.

No one on East Flamingo Road that night—including Suge Knight—admitted to seeing anything that aided investigators in their efforts to find the killer or accomplices. Police assumed that Suge Knight, who was driving the car and sitting next to Tupac, would probably be their best eyewitness. They were wrong.

Petersen said, "He's obviously a prime witness in this, also a victim, and we've gotten no cooperation from him. We believe we know who's responsible for this. The problem we have with this case is we don't have anyone willing to come forward and testify to it. The gangster-rap mentality that they don't want to talk to police is definitely hurting this case."

Sergeant Kevin Manning agreed. "He doesn't care. It's the code of that mentality. They just don't care."

When Suge Knight was asked by an ABC "Prime Time Live" reporter whether he would tell the police who killed Tupac if he knew who it was, he answered slowly but directly, "Ab-so-lute-ly not. I mean, because I don't know. It's not my job. I don't get paid to solve homicides. I don't get paid to tell on people."

"There's a potential for God knows how many witnesses that night," Lieutenant Petersen commented. "It was a Saturday night. It was a fight night. It was close to the Strip.

"How many hundreds of people were at that intersection? Say there were a hundred. Nobody was able to provide us with an accurate description of the shooter and the vehicle?"

The best anyone on the scene could tell investigators was that the Cadillac was light-colored, probably white.

"Most of the witnesses said the car was white," Petersen confirmed. "How many white Cadillacs are there in this town?"

Investigators were also given what they called "misinformation," by "unreliable sources," that everyone in the Cadillac was wearing masks. But that didn't correspond with a claim by the lone potentially cooperative witness, Yafeu Fula, who claimed he could possibly ID the gunman, whose face he said wasn't covered.

Early in the Shakur investigation, Sergeant Manning told a reporter, "The shooting was not a random act of violence."

But that's about all investigators seemed sure of.

Perhaps most frustrating, the members of the entourage were quiet about the shooting, claiming they only saw the Cadillac and not the assailants. Several bodyguards were in the group, and their lack of detailed information took Metro investigators by surprise. After all, they were being paid to protect Tupac and Suge.

"It amazes me," Kevin Manning said, "when they have professional bodyguards who can't even give us an accurate description of the vehicle. You'd think a personal bodyguard would have seen something. It's a murder, and the people closest to the scene should be able to help us, but they say they didn't see anything. So far they haven't enlightened us as to a suspect or a motive, and that's the bottom line."

The night of the shooting, about eight detectives were on the scene, Petersen said, including general-assignment detectives, a watch commander, and patrol officers "trying to deal with the mass of witnesses and the large crime scene."

One crime-scene analyst was called because it was an "attempted homicide," said Lieutenant Brad Simpson, who oversees Metro's criminalistics section. "[Tupac] didn't die right away, or we would have sent two technicians. We approached it as an attempted homicide, so we only sent one senior crime-scene analyst."

"On average there are a minimum of two, probably three, criminalists on a homicide scene," he said. "One is a crime-scene supervisor and one a senior crime-scene analyst, which means they've been on [the job] for at least four years. Their job is to collect the forensics evidence. In the Tupac Shakur case, they would look at the bullet holes in the vehicle, the trajectory of the bullet holes hitting the car and him, blood-splatter evidence, which shows the direction of high-velocity wounds. They would photograph the crime scene, taking overall views. They would probably go back within a week to take an aerial shot to get a better perspective of what's going on. They would diagram the crime scene."

An aerial photograph was never taken. (Aerial photos are used for court. If there's an arrest, photos of the street will be taken from a helicopter. The police didn't take an aerial photo that night "because it was dark," Manning claimed.)

A Metro K-9 (canine) team was dispatched to the Strip and Harmon Avenue to search for a gun police believed may have been thrown into the center divider. Later that night, however, they learned that the shooting took place a mile away. So the dogs were sniffing for 15 minutes in the wrong place. A helicopter (Metro has three) wasn't used in the investigation to search for the Cadillac, because by the time the police realized where the shooting had taken place, too much time had elapsed to dispatch a helicopter. They figured the getaway car was long gone.

When investigators learned that the gunman fled south on Koval Lane, detectives checked to see if any shootings had occurred in that area; there were no reports of any. And no fights or disturbances were reported involving black men in a Cadillac.

A Nevada Highway Patrol sergeant and six troopers arrived at Harmon where Suge's BMW came to a halt and blocked the Strip to through traffic.

"We got a call that shots were fired on the Strip," trooper Steve Harney explained, "that there was a shooting in progress. When we first arrived we shut everything down. We have to shut everything down in case there are any bad guys around."

Ironically, Suge's escape route had taken the BMW almost all the way back to the MGM Grand, where the state troopers' presence was already heavy because of the Tyson-Seldon fight.

"Look at how many additional people were there because of the fight. So many officers responded because there were hundreds working that night. We have what's called an operational plan," Harney said. "Any time there's a major event on the Strip, the hotels involved hire additional officers, and we provide traffic control. When there's a shooting, it's a simultaneous notification to Metro and the highway patrol. We stayed on all night."

Bicycle patrol officer Michael McDonald, who works the swing shift as a cop and serves as an elected Las Vegas City Councilman by day, was called to the scene as backup. "We rolled on it as soon as we heard they had a shooting going on," McDonald explained. McDonald and his partner, officer Eric Holyoak, were up the Strip near the Circus Circus casino.

"I was at a car stop. You just start rolling. You don't have time to think about it. I didn't even finish the stop. I gave [the driver] his stuff back, his license and registration, said 'See you later, bye,' and I was outta there."

He said officers knew right away that it was Tupac Shakur bleeding to death inside the BMW.

By the time McDonald arrived on the scene a few minutes after the BMW was stopped, "The whole cavalry had arrived. There must have been thirty or forty patrol cars," he said. "When we got there, the ambulances were just leaving."

"I had to calm the bodyguards down," McDonald said. "They were saying, 'Man, we have to go to the hospital with 'Pac.' They were freaking out. Their friend had just been shot. They were upset. I talked to them. I told them that if they didn't calm down, the cops were going to have to cuff them and take them in. I made sure they didn't mingle. The detectives don't want the witnesses to speak to each other. I told them, 'You guys have to understand, the quicker you talk to the detectives, the quicker you're outta here.' I said, 'You can do this here or you can do this downtown.' They calmed down. After the detectives talked to them, they all jumped in their cars and went to the hospital.

"They were in three cars," McDonald continued. "Their cars were parked in the middle of the street, right next to the median. When the BMW came to rest, it was in the middle of the intersection at Harmon and the Boulevard. It was facing kind of southeast, turned to the left, cocked, like Knight was in the middle of making a left turn when he was stopped. It had four flat tires. The rims were bent from going over the curbs."

No one knows where Suge was heading by trying to make the left turn onto Harmon from the Strip.

Dispatch had called detectives from general assignment to investigate before a homicide team was called in. Detectives arrived and began interviewing the witnesses. But the scene was chaotic. Everyone on the street knew it was Tupac. He was easily recognized by music and film fans. A large crowd gathered. People began charging the car, trying to rip off the side-view mirrors, wire-rimmed hubcaps, door handles—anything they could grab. The cops yelled at them to get back and threatened to arrest anyone who got near the car. A few officers had to physically keep people back. It was the scene of an attempted homicide (at the least) and the car was evidence. The police, including officers McDonald and Holyoak, secured the perimeter, protecting the crime scene, until investigators and crime analysts were finished working it.

Malcolm Payne, chief photographer for the *Herald Dispatch* newspaper in South Central Los Angeles, was on assignment in Las Vegas covering the Tyson fight, and had returned to his hotel room at the Aladdin Hotel across the street from where the BMW came to rest. He looked out his window to the street scene below.

"I saw the yellow tape and police and realized there had

to be a murder or something," he said. "I grabbed my camera and went down there."

When he got to the street, he asked what happened. "A little boy told me, 'Tupac got killed.' He said, 'That's the car he was riding in.'

"Immediately, what went through my head was the scene out of 'Bonnie and Clyde.' The car was all shot up. I said to myself that this was history and I was going to shoot it. So I pulled out my camera and started taking pictures. Tupac was like a legend, and it was his last ride, you know?"

Payne began shooting photos of the car, riddled with bullet holes, and of the witnesses from Tupac's entourage as they were being interviewed by detectives. Yellow crime-scene tape separated the witnesses from the crowd gathered on the street. The street was closed; police had blocked off the Strip to through traffic.

"The ambulance was gone," Payne said. "I got a shot of some of the guys. They were upset. I shot them sitting on the sidewalk. The police had them blocked off with yellow tape. They kept them there for quite some time, at least two hours. Their cars were right there, on the side [of the road].

"When I got there the street was blocked off. You had plainclothes, uniforms, and the guys who ride around Vegas on bicycles. And they'd brought out a dog team. Somebody told them the gun was thrown out in the median, so they had the dogs out searching in the median for the gun. It seemed like the police were trying to do a thorough investigation at that crime scene. They were really trying to find the gun. They were tearing that car up too."

Payne turned out to be the only still photographer at the crime scene. The police took still photographs, but theirs weren't taken for public consumption, and have been locked away in a file cabinet inside Metro's photo lab with a "420" (murder) label.

Officer Michael McDonald said that when the detectives arrived, they investigated three different scenes: the shooting at Flamingo and Koval; the left turn from Flamingo onto the Strip; and the center divider where Suge's car stopped for good. They also backtracked to make sure there weren't any casings somewhere else.

"Everybody locked down the scene. When you know it's a blatant homicide, you lock the scene down till detectives can get there. You put cones over the casings, cordon off the crime scene, put the tape up, keep witnesses from talking to each other. We were there for hours, way into overtime," McDonald said.

Once the street was reopened to one lane, officers stopped some drivers to question them. They were looking for witnesses. They found none. Reports that cops were stopping only black male drivers were untrue, said NHP trooper Steve Harney and Metro bike cop Michael McDonald, both of whom were there when motorists were being stopped.

"We do not do that," Harney said. "When we did stop people to question them, we stopped everybody. It wasn't just black male adults. We treat everybody the same."

Unlike the location where the BMW came to rest, the shooting scene at Flamingo and Koval in front of the Maxim wasn't secured right away.

"It made it tougher" to investigate, Sergeant Kevin Manning admitted later. "Within a relatively short period of time, that scene was secured enough so that there was still evidence present. But if any of it had been moved, like cars hitting it, how do we know?"

State trooper Steve Harney added, "You've got to understand, when it's a shooting, unless it's in a house, if you're on an interstate or a busy street, you're not going to have as much preservation of evidence."

When the K-9 unit arrived, it went to work a mile away, where Suge and Tupac ended up, not at the crime scene where the shooting actually took place. The police still believed the gunfire had occurred on the Strip. Had police talked to the members of the entourage immediately, they might have told them that the Cadillac had fled, and which way it'd gone. But by the time the general-assignment detectives arrived and began questioning them, not only had enough time gone by for the Cadillac to flee without a trace, but the entourage witnesses were irate.

Detectives were surprised when members of the entourage who'd witnessed the shooting wouldn't talk. They weren't willing to give up any information at all after the patrol cops had thrown them face down on the street's blacktop. They made it very clear afterwards that they were angry with the way the officers treated them. Though Metro police called it standard procedure, when its officers treated potential witnesses to the highest-profile murder case in the history of the department like suspected criminals, they forever alienated the all-important members of the entourage, including Suge Knight. All hope of establishing cooperation from the witnesses vanished in those first few minutes. Metro gained nothing and lost everything.

Detectives eventually questioned witnesses from the first crime scene about the actual shooting. They talked some, but not a lot—and there were inconsistencies. Some witnesses told detectives the Cadillac had California license plates. Others said Nevada. No one was sure. In addition, there were early reports that the shooters were women, but according to Metro Lieutenant Larry Spinosa, that's not what the police ultimately concluded. People on the street that night may have been referring to the women who were in the Chrysler sedan near Suge's BMW when the shots were fired.

According to Kevin Manning, when detectives arrived at the scene of the shooting, the four women were still there. They were escorted to an interview room at Metro Police's headquarters downtown, in Las Vegas City Hall on Stewart Avenue and Las Vegas Boulevard. The women, who were from California, were not planted at the intersection to set up Tupac and Suge, nor were they used as distractions while the gunman drove up in the Cadillac, Manning insisted. It was a coincidence. The women claimed they didn't see the shooter. Their names have not been released.

Detective Brent Becker agreed that the women were not vital to the investigation. "They were just people in the mess," he said. "They're just like everybody else who was on the street that night. There were a lot of women nearby. There's no significance. I'd sure hate to hear about four women getting jammed up because someone thinks they're strong witnesses."

Most of the witnesses, including bystanders on the street, told the officers it looked like there were four men, all African-American, inside the four-door Cadillac. Witnesses also told police that no one in the Cadillac got out, that the shots were fired from inside the car, probably from the back seat. Some later reports had one gunman getting out and tracking Tupac, aiming directly for his side of the car, but police have said that wasn't the case.

And then there were the witnesses who were in the cars behind Tupac when the shooting erupted. Several from Tupac's entourage were taken downtown by general-assignment detectives early the next morning for questioning, according to Becker, instead of being interviewed on the street. Bodyguard Frank Alexander and rapper Malcolm Greenridge were in the car behind Tupac and Suge. Alexander and Greenridge told police they didn't see anything. Later, they recanted their stories, telling the *Los Angeles Times* that homicide detectives never asked them if they could identify the shooter.

Nineteen-year-old Yafeu Fula, a member of Outlaw Immortalz, a back-up rap group that toured with Tupac, was the third man in the car with Alexander and Greenridge. He was interviewed briefly on the street that night by homicide detectives. He told them he would probably be able to pick out the shooter from a photo line-up of suspects. Police took his name and telephone number. He was the best eyewitness police talked to that night. Of all the potential witnesses to the shooting, only Yafeu Fula claimed to have seen anything.

No one else was able, or willing, to help.

Within 48 hours of the shooting, on the following Monday, Las Vegas police called what would be their only news conference on the subject of Tupac Shakur. The national media, as well as local print, radio, and broadcast journalists, attended. What made the conference unusual were the entertainment reporters standing shoulder to shoulder with the hard-news reporters who are accustomed to following and reporting on homicides.

Sergeant Manning, along with Sergeant Greg McCurdy from Metro's Public Affairs Office, held the news briefing on the lawn next to the executive-park building on West Charleston Boulevard that houses homicide's offices. With the cameras and mikes aimed at him, Manning stood in the shade of the trees to evade the blazing midday sun. By afternoon, the temperature had soared to nearly 100 degrees.

He read a brief statement—his original press release of the shooting—then fielded questions from reporters. For some, it would be the only opportunity they would have to speak directly to the sergeant. Most of the reporters' questions were about the assailant; some asked about Tupac's condition. One asked about the gun.

"We have not and will not make any comments about the gun. It's the only real physical evidence we have," Sergeant Manning said, referring to information that ballistics uncovered from the shell casings and bullets. "I know what's out there [in the media]. Semiautomatic would be accurate. Glock [a semiautomatic Glock pistol] has been mentioned. We don't know where the Glock is coming from. We have never said that."

In response to a reporter's question, Manning addressed the rumor that Suge Knight, not Tupac, was the intended target, by saying that they were not based on the facts of the case. "The gunfire hit the passenger and the passenger side," he said. "I assume the passenger was the target."

Several reporters walked up to Manning after his news conference and handed him their business cards, asking to be faxed or called if anything new came up. The homicide sergeant wasn't happy "dealing"—as he called it—with reporters. They were a nuisance and didn't serve his purposes. Later, Manning complained that interruptions from reporters were what kept him from investigating the murder.

The feeling at Metro toward the media has sometimes tended toward disdain and mistrust. When reporters call to ask about a crime or an internal investigation into misconduct by an officer, they're often met with remarks like, "That's old news; why are you asking about that?" or "That's not a story." The thinking inside Metro's homicide unit (and, for that matter, other units at Metro) is that they should only answer questions from reporters if it serves Metro's investigation purposes. Considerations of "the public's right to know," often with even the most basic information, have traditionally taken a back seat.

Over the next few weeks, with international media attention focused on the shooting and death of Tupac Shakur, detectives Becker and Franks would go on camera only once, making an appearance on the Fox Network's "America's Most Wanted" television show. But Sergeant Manning wouldn't allow the partners to be interviewed on camera—or off—by "Unsolved Mysteries" when producers from Burbank, California, came to town to produce their own segment about the murder.

"They can't help us," Manning explained. "It would be of no use to us in our investigation." The decision was made despite the fact that "Unsolved" claimed to have more viewers than "America's Most Wanted" and a better "solve rate." According to an "Unsolved Mysteries" producer, one of the reasons detectives declined was because "Unsolved" also airs what the producer called their "ugga bugga stories," such as UFO sightings and tales of spontaneous human combustion, sandwiched between true unsolved crime stories. "America's

Most Wanted" reports only crime and missing-persons stories.

Regardless of the real reason for Metro's non-participation, it turned out to be a lost opportunity. After the "Unsolved Mysteries" piece aired on March 14, 1997—without cop interviews—the show received hundreds of tips. One, from a woman who said she was told twice by a friend that he committed the murder, appeared to be solid. The woman, living in a Southern state, was afraid to give her name. An FBI agent who was in the "Unsolved Mysteries" studio when the program aired interviewed the woman and spent a lot of time with her on the phone. Metro Police were not in the studio, having declined when asked to go to Burbank to be on hand in case any solid tips were called in.

Metro detectives had one willing witness, 19-year-old Yafeu Fula, a rapper from New Jersey, who watched the shooting from the car behind Suge's and claimed he'd be able to pick the gunman out of a photo lineup. But instead of detaining him until they could question him in depth, police let Fula go.

Almost immediately after being allowed to leave Las Vegas, Fula contacted a lawyer, David Kenner, Death Row's attorney. Kenner played hard to get with Las Vegas investigators for two months. Promises to set up a meeting between detectives and Fula were made, but never kept.

It may have been fear that prompted Fula to enlist Death Row's lawyer to keep him from being interviewed by Las Vegas police. After all, had he talked, identifying the shooter, he would have been a snitch; people would find that out during the trial of whomever he fingered, if not before. Fula, it turns out, had good reason to be frightened. Two months, almost to the day after Tupac was shot, the lead witness to the shooting was forever gagged—Yafeu Fula was murdered in New Jersey.

• • •

Detectives' hopes for a break in the case were raised four months after the death of Yafeu Fula when Frank Alexander and Malcolm Greenridge, bodyguards who were in the car with Fula, came forward, telling a *Los Angeles Times* reporter that they might be able to identify the shooter. The pair, however, criticized Las Vegas police, claiming Metro detectives never asked them to look at photos of possible suspects when investigators questioned them on the night of the shooting.

Both men said they had come forward six months later because they were tired of hearing Las Vegas police say that an arrest had not been made because of uncooperative witnesses, the *L.A. Times* reported. They also said that Metro Police had not contacted them since their questioning the night of the shooting. Like other witnesses, the pair complained that they were offended that night by the tactics of the cops, who made them lie face down on the ground after ordering them out of their cars, then held them for two hours before they were questioned by detectives.

Sergeant Manning said the two might be able to help crack the case, while also saying that if they did, they'd be changing their stories from what they originally told detectives. According to Manning, when Alexander was asked on the night of the shooting if he could identify the gunman, he replied, "Absolutely not." Greenridge, when asked by detectives if he could identify the gunman, answered, "Nope." Alexander's original interview was 13 pages long after it was transcribed, Greenridge's was 11. They consisted mostly of descriptions of the night's events, without too many specifics.

"They never said they could identify a shooter," Manning said. "Nowhere during the [initial] taped interview did they say they could recognize or identify anyone in the vehicle, the shooter or otherwise." Manning commented that it was curious the pair complained to a *Los Angeles Times* reporter that they were harassed by police, but also said they were never contacted by detectives. "So which is it?" Manning asked.

Detectives Becker and Franks went to California after the *L.A. Times'* story appeared so they could reinterview Alexander and Greenridge. Alexander met with the detectives at an Orange County restaurant, where he told them the *L.A. Times* story was "exaggerated" and denied saying he could identify the shooter, Manning said. He viewed suspects from photographs—what cops refer to as a photo lineup—but he couldn't pick out the gunman.

Greenridge, interviewed the same day as Alexander at another location, also told Becker and Franks that he could not identify the shooter. He told the detectives he didn't even want to look at the photos.

"We recontacted them and Greenridge stated, 'I still say I didn't see anything,'" Petersen explained. "These guys are responsible for Shakur's safety and well being, and the shooting goes down and they don't get an accurate description of the vehicle. When bullets are flying, who knows what they saw? If anybody out there did see it and didn't tell us what they saw that night or within a reasonable period after, then they basically screwed us out of a prosecution."

Lieutenant Petersen emphasized that even if the pair had said they could positively identify the assailant, defense attorneys would ask them, "How does your recollection of what happened get better six months after the event?"

"All it did was cause a lot of problems," Manning said in a published interview, "problems with everybody thinking we didn't do what we were supposed to do, and having us have to chase Frank Alexander and Malcolm Greenridge down."

The investigators called it a wasted trip and a waste of their time. They ended up back where they had started.

• • •

The problems weren't all coming from the outside. During the first week of the investigation, detectives thought they'd found help from one of their own in identifying members of Tupac's entourage videotaped during the scuffle by the MGM Grand's surveillance camera.

"They got a call from a young black Metro patrolman," an anonymous police source said. "He told them he knew some of the people and could help identify some of them. It turns out he didn't identify any of them. They think he came in to see what they had... he left homicide and got into a brand-spanking-new Lexus."

The source claimed investigators believed he might have been a snake, an informant for those wanting to plant someone inside the investigation.

Besides the possible betrayal by one of their own, Las Vegas police also had to watch their backs with out-of-town police officers as well, who might have alliances with gang members.

"Every step of this investigation everybody had to be careful," the same police source said. "These guys [rappers] employ tons of cops."

"When this thing hit here, right away the Los Angeles agency down there called and said, 'Hey, we want to help.' All they wanted to do was pick their brains for information."

An L.A.P.D. detective, who spoke on the condition that his name not be used, said he didn't believe that Metro and L.A. police don't trust each other, but that they have to protect their information.

"Those kinds of things go on all the time between agencies," he said. "Everybody's protecting their information. These are high-profile cases and nobody wants to make a mistake. I don't know if there's distrust [from Metro]. When all your witnesses live in Los Angeles, it makes it difficult logistically to investigate it in Las Vegas."

New York City police also called homicide detectives in Las Vegas looking for information. Sergeant Manning had called them to talk about the first time Tupac was shot, in Manhattan in 1994.

"We talked to numerous people in New York," Manning said. "The thing that was interesting, every time I talked to someone in New York, I asked, 'Who's case is this?' I talked to someone who said it was his case, then I'd call back and someone else would say it's their case. I finally asked a lieutenant to help straighten it out. I couldn't believe they had all these guys in charge of this investigation. The funny thing was, they stopped calling me back after that. Most of them seemed to be on fishing expeditions rather than trying to find out [information] for their investigation. I couldn't hazard a guess why."

On the other hand, another source said, "Compton [police], without even asking, sent a six-man investigative team made up of L.A. County Sheriff's Department and Compton P.D. [to Las Vegas]. They were very helpful. They shared information as to who in law enforcement to be leery of, who was working for [various] gang members." The officers spent two days with homicide investigators in Las Vegas.

A law-enforcement agent elaborated on the dynamics of protecting police investigations from infiltration. "In traditional organized crime investigations, the old La Cosa Nostra kinds of investigations, police always had to be leery of outside officers until they knew the answers, because that was a very common way for bad guys to get information. If you're a successful bad guy, you try to develop sources in the good-guy community, that being law enforcement. It's a possibility [in the Tupac investigation]. It's always been that way."

The fact that it was still that way during the investigation into Tupac's murder was underscored by a peculiar incident in Los Angeles in March 1997. Detective Frank J. Lyga, an undercover police officer wearing civilian clothes and driving an unmarked police car, radioed to his fellow officers that he was being followed and harassed by a motorist who, it turned out, was also an out-of-uniform off-duty cop, officer Kevin L. Gaines.

The *Los Angeles Times* reported that the altercation began with Lyga and Gaines staring each other down at a red light. It then escalated into a verbal confrontation.

An unnamed source close to the investigation told the *Los Angeles Daily News* that Gaines rolled down the window of his car. A published report stated that he told Lyga to quit staring him down or he would shoot him.

That's when Lyga drove away and radioed dispatchers that he was having trouble with the motorist, the *L.A. Times* reported. A few blocks later, the officers were again next to each other at a traffic light.

Gaines pulled a handgun on Lyga, who "feared he was about to be shot," Lyga told investigators. Lyga pulled his department weapon and fired twice, fatally wounding Gaines, L.A.P.D. Lt. Anthony Alba told *The Associated Press*. Gaines didn't know Lyga was an officer and Lyga didn't know Gaines was an officer until Gaines was taken to a hospital, where he died. Gaines' family expressed serious doubts that Kevin Gaines provoked the shooting because, they claimed, he wasn't the type.

After the shooting, it was revealed that Gaines, a six-year veteran of the L.A.P.D., had been dating and living with Suge's estranged wife, Sharitha Golden Knight. The officer was driving Sharitha's car when the altercation occurred. It was also revealed that in an earlier incident, Gaines reported to Internal Affairs that officers pushed and cuffed him on August 16, 1996, when they searched a home owned by Sharitha Knight.

Kevin Gaines' widow, who was separated from her husband at the time of his death, hired Johnnie Cochran Jr., O.J. Simpson's former criminal defense lawyer, to investigate the homicide.

While the Suge Knight connection is intriguing, police have claimed that there was no harassment and that the Suge association was irrelevant.

• • •

False tips are a regular occurrence in any murder case. In a big murder case, they can become a serious nuisance, and the Tupac Shakur case was no exception.

On the morning of March 26, 1997, a man came forward and told homicide detectives that he'd seen everything and could identify the gunman. The man's story deteriorated during interviews, until he finally confessed that he wasn't even in Las Vegas at the time.

Sergeant Kevin Manning said a few "whackos" called in to "confess." One man left a blow-by-blow confession with minute and descriptive details on homicide's voice mail. There was only one problem. He claimed he did it in December, two months *after* Tupac was killed.

Another "informant" who was in custody on another charge in Wisconsin swore to police there that he knew who shot Tupac Shakur. He gave the cops specific information on the investigation, "specifics we were looking for," Manning said. "Police there interviewed the guy. They did a diagram of the crime. He was supposed to be a witness. They faxed his statement to us."

What police in Las Vegas got, however, was a script from the "Unsolved Mysteries" segment about Tupac's murder that aired in March 1997.

"He copied 'Unsolved Mysteries' word for word," Manning said. "We continue to get hundreds and hundreds of calls from 'America's Most Wanted' and 'Unsolved Mysteries.' If they [callers] have too many details, how do we sort out the credible from the uncredible?"

That's why, Manning continued, police don't worry about incorrect and inaccurate information circulating, because it helps them tell the real witnesses from the fakes.

Some evidence remains sacrosanct. The gun, for example. The only hard evidence police have is from the ballistics. And they won't give up that information to the media, because only the perpetrators and the cops know the truth. That piece of intelligence was useful when a tip came in on April 11, 1997, from FBI agents in Bakersfield, California. Sergeant Manning tells the story:

"We got a call from the FBI in Bakersfield who had a guy who said he was in the car with the shooter, but he would only talk to an FBI agent. No one else. No other law enforcement. So I said, 'Okay.' We gave them some questions to ask. It turned out to be nothing. The guy said he shot into the driver's side with an Uzi."

Police haven't disclosed what kind of gun shot Tupac, but it's fairly obvious that it wasn't an Uzi or an assault weapon, which would have caused considerably more damage to the car and more serious injuries to Suge Knight.

Even if a gun were recovered, Manning said, "We would still have difficulty putting that weapon in the actual shooter's possession. By now it's been too long. Even with fingerprints, it wouldn't be too useful."

In fact, he added, "Even a confession wouldn't solve the case—without concrete physical evidence."

Reports that there was more than one gunman were not true, Manning added. Also, reports that one gunman got out of the car to shoot Tupac were unfounded. The security guards and some of the members of the entourage got out of their cars, and witnesses in the confusion might have thought that one of *them* was the shooter, Manning said.

Richard Fischbein, the Manhattan attorney administering Shakur's million-dollar estate and representing Tupac's mother, said in a telephone interview, "It's an outrage that the Las Vegas police are sitting around waiting for a suspect to come to them. I believe that had [Afeni] been anyone else, they would have had the courtesy to call her, to keep in contact to tell her what is going on.

"Afeni's comment is, it's not going to bring her son back

if they catch the killers or they don't catch them. On the other hand, it would be nice if the Las Vegas Police Department tried, because that would be the right thing to do. It would show that it doesn't matter who you are—if you get shot, the police are going to be there to do something about it."

But homicide Lieutenant Petersen takes issue with the statement, saying Shakur's mother, when contacted by detectives, refused to talk to them.

"The first time we contacted Mrs. Shakur, she would not talk to us. All other contacts were made through her attorney," Petersen responded.

A local radio personality intimated prejudice, saying that if Tupac hadn't been a gangsta rapper, police might have worked harder to solve the case. Louis Conner, a deejay for KCEP radio in Las Vegas whose on-air name is LC, played Tupac's music the remainder of the day that Tupac passed away—"as a tribute to him." He said he doesn't understand why police haven't made progress in their investigation.

"It's unfortunate" that Metro Police have not been able to make an arrest in the Shakur case, LC said months after Tupac's murder. "Maybe they're out of manpower, I don't know. I don't think it's a black and white issue. I think it's what Tupac represented, what he rapped about in his music. I think that makes it another type of prejudice. A lot of prejudices and stereotypes went into this case, and that's one of the things holding up the investigation process. I think they're working on it. They're just going about it at their own pace."

Sway, a disk jockey on San Francisco's KMEL, agreed that police could do more in attempting to find Tupac's killer.

In an interview from his San Francisco studio, Sway said, "This is hard for me to believe—that somebody as visible as Tupac can, during prime time in Las Vegas, just get massacred on the Strip. It doesn't seem like that's possible in nineteen-ninety-seven without somebody knowing something.

"I don't think the powers that be give a damn that another little ghetto kid gets killed in the streets. It's not important to them to solve this case. I think they feel it's another headache killed in the streets. It doesn't serve their time and energy to solve the case of Tupac Shakur. I think it's just another day in America. If it was one of theirs, the killer probably would have been convicted and sentenced to death by now. From what Tupac represented to them, they probably thought it didn't matter as much."

Orlando "Little Lando" Anderson's name surfaced early in the investigation, when it was determined that he was the one attacked by Tupac and members of his entourage at the MGM Grand just hours before the mortal drive-by shooting. And police have said Anderson appears to be associated with the Crips, the rival street gang to the Bloods, with which Suge Knight is allegedly affiliated. Detectives, however, have stopped just short of calling Anderson an actual suspect.

"We're not ruling anybody out at this time," Lieutenant Petersen told The Associated Press, "but for us to say he's the only suspect is incorrect. There are people out there who believe Marion Knight is a suspect."

Homicide detectives don't keep lists with names of suspects, Petersen said. It's others, he claimed, not the cops, who have called Anderson a suspect.

Police treaded lightly for another reason, a good one. "I'm getting tired of everybody calling Orlando Anderson a suspect," Detective Becker said, "because if he gets killed..."

While police claim that no one will come forward and point a finger at the gunman, they, too, refuse to officially name the shooter even while they say they think they know who did it.

Sergeant Manning said, "We'd like to solve every case. In this particular case, there's personal pride and organizational pride involved. We'd love to put handcuffs on somebody. Once again, it comes back to this: until somebody has the courage to take the witness stand and put themselves in front of the prosecution and defense attorneys to answer hard questions, the case is at a standstill. This isn't like you have fiber evidence and hair evidence. You're talking about a drive-by shooting that leaves very little evidence behind."

Compton Mayor Omar Bradley said Compton cops have expressed to him their disappointment in Metro's handling of Orlando Anderson after they arrested him. Officers told him that the word on the street with gang members was that Anderson was somehow involved.

"Officers don't like to criticize each other publicly," Bradley said. "But they did criticize Las Vegas police privately.

"We arrested someone [in the Shakur case]," the mayor said. "The Las Vegas police didn't want him. Compton police thought he was the one. I think the Compton police did their job."

Bradley said he was surprised that Anderson "was not further scrutinized by the Las Vegas Police Department. I don't understand why the Las Vegas police didn't pursue the case. It doesn't seem as if the investigation is proceeding."

When told that Las Vegas investigators felt they didn't have enough evidence to charge Anderson with Shakur's murder, Bradley said, "Evidence is something that prosecutors would decide, isn't it? Did Metro submit their case to the district attorney?"

The answer to that question is no.

"We believe we know who is responsible for this," Lieutenant Wayne Petersen added. "The problem we have with this case is we don't have anyone willing to come forward and testify to it. The gang, gangster-rap mentality that they don't want to tell the police is definitely hurting this case. We don't have any more than rumor and innuendo. It's all these unconfirmed sources saying that, yes, Orlando Anderson did it, but there's no witness there (at the scene) who can testify to it. It's the old talk on the street, everybody claiming they heard that Orlando Anderson did it. We have no evidence linking him to this."

Petersen, the lieutenant in charge of the homicide division of the Las Vegas Metropolitan Police Department, summed it up. "Getting away with murder happens all the time. The general public would probably be alarmed to know how often people get away with murder."

The list of questionable decisions in the Tupac Shakur homicide investigation is long.

Both bike cops who heard the shooting from the Maxim Hotel garage followed the BMW instead of splitting up so one could secure the crime scene.

Detectives and a K-9 team were dispatched to the wrong location.

No aerial photos were taken.

Metro police who responded to the bike cops' calls for back-up alienated all but one of the potential witnesses within a few minutes of the shooting.

Detectives released Yafeu Fula—the only witness willing to cooperate. This decision becomes even more questionable in light of Fula's murder two months later, before police could interview him. When Metro needs prostitutes or transients or even out-of-towners to testify as witnesses or to issue statements against a suspect, they simply lock them up, because they're considered flight risks. Even though the other witnesses to Tupac's shooting were uncooperative, police didn't feel they needed to detain their only willing witness. Yafeu Fula slipped through their fingers.

Metro detectives, while saying they were doing the best they could to investigate the murder, admitted waiting for their phones to ring. Yet, when their phones did ring, they often chalked up the calls to fake leads from wannabe tipsters. When Sergeant Manning received 300 calls in one day about the Shakur case, he simply stopped answering his phone and let his recorder pick them up.

The detectives assigned to the Shakur murder appeared on "America's Most Wanted," but not "Unsolved Mysteries." News stories historically prompt witnesses to come forward, and sometimes ferret out suspects. Publicity via the media gets the word out to the public, which, in turn, sometimes helps solve crimes. Not only would Metro not take part in the "Unsolved Mysteries" segment, they declined to be on hand to take calls at the studio right after "Unsolved Mysteries" aired.

Finally, Metro police have said they believe they've known all along who the killer is, but they don't have enough evidence to press charges. If they do know who's behind the killing, any efforts they've made to capitalize on that knowledge have been ineffectual.

5

ABOUT TUPAC SHAKUR

Violence was nothing new to Tupac Shakur. Tupac grew up on the mean streets of New York City. A product of that environment, as an adult he looked every inch the thug his songs insisted he was.

His head was clean shaven, his muscular six-foot 215-pound frame was covered in tattoos. Even after surviving an earlier shooting, he was able to maintain rippled abdominal muscles that resembled a washboard.

He was handsome, with boyish good looks and an engaging smile and manner. He had a sauntering but determined walk, a hard stare but soft eyes and long eyelashes—a look decidedly different from other rappers.

Over the years, Tupac had accumulated more than a handful of tattoos. The one on his left forearm said "OUT-LAW." On his right upper arm was the word "HEARTLESS" etched above a bloody skull and crossbones. On his back was "Exodus 18.11" ("Now I know that the Lord is greater than all gods: For in the thing wherein they dealt proudly he *was* above them.").

He also had the image of an AK-47 semiautomatic assault weapon tattooed on his left upper chest just below a scar from a bullet wound. The tattoo splashed across Tupac's lower chest said "THUG LIFE" with a bullet in place of the letter "I." Above that was "50 NIGGAZ" positioned atop a rifle. This tattoo symbolized a black confederation among the fifty U.S. states. And splashing the word "Nigga" on his chest, he believed, would advertise it as an acronym, which he claimed meant "Never Ignorant Getting Goals Accomplished." "2PAC," his stage name, was tattooed on his left breast. And on his right upper chest was "2DIE4" below the profile of an African-American woman's face. Some believe it was a portrait of his mother.

The images tattooed on his body represented the things that Tupac held sacred.

Tupac also adorned himself with jewelry. He had a particular penchant for gold. Besides the solid-gold chains around his neck, and diamond and gold rings on fingers of both hands, he wore diamond studs in his nose and ears and an 18-karat-gold Rolex watch on his right wrist.

Tupac wore jewelry like medals, badges of honor. To his director in his first movie, *Juice,* he recited Robert Frost's poem "Nothing Gold Can Stay." Even the lyrics of Tupac's favorite passage, a borrowed poem, became a reality for him. It read:

"Nature's first green is gold, her hardest hue to hold. Her early leaves aflower; but only so an hour. Leaf subsides to leaf. So Eden sank to grief, so dawn goes down today. Nothing gold can stay." (Tupac, who was an avid reader, often quoted passages from a book or lines from a poem or lyrics from a song. His friends were used to it. He'd done it since he was a kid.)

Just before his death, Tupac formed a new group made up of kids, which he named Nothing Gold. He planned to personally produce their songs, which would, he felt, send a positive message to teenagers.

Tupac was a talented singer-songwriter with five solo albums to his name. Additionally, Tupac contributed songs to soundtracks for several movies, including *Above the Rim, Poetic Justice, The Show, Supercop,* and *Sunset Park.* He was also a rising film star, having starred in the movies *Juice* (1992),

Poetic Justice (1993) with Janet Jackson, *Bullet, Above the Rim, Gridlock'd,* and *Gang Related,* which wrapped up a week before the fatal shooting and was to be released on the first anniversary of his death.

Tupac had quite a following. Fans lined up for hours at record stores in Las Vegas awaiting the November 5, 1996, midnight release of Tupac's last album, *Don Killuminati—The 7-Day Theory,* released posthumously. The day before, Mike Tyson, accompanied by several men, tried to buy the CD a day early from Tower Records' Wow store on West Sahara Avenue, about 10 miles from his Las Vegas mansion.

"He didn't believe us when we told him it wasn't available yet," said the store clerk who waited on him. "We told him, 'Come back tomorrow.'" Tyson did return the next day to purchase his CD.

Boston Globe movie critic Jay Carr described Shakur's acting abilities in a January 31, 1997 review. "Whatever else the late gangsta rapper Tupac Shakur was, he was a good movie actor," Carr wrote. "He was good in *Juice,* and he was the best thing in *Poetic Justice.* He's even more appealing as the soulful half of the strung-out buddy team alongside Tim Roth in *Gridlock'd.*"

According to rap journalist Kevin Powell, Tupac acted "with a moody intensity comparable to that of James Dean," whose acting career was also cut short, but by a fatal car accident.

Tupac had reason to be moody. His childhood had been far from easy.

Tupac's mother, Alice Faye Williams, aka Afeni Shakur, and his father, Billy Garland, were founding members of the national Black Panther Party, based in New York, in the late 1960s. Alice, while out on bail pending felony charges for conspiring to blow up department stores and police stations, dated Garland. Alice earlier had been married to Lumumba Abdul Shakur, but when she got pregnant (by Garland), Lumumba, a fellow Panther, divorced her a short time later.

In April 1969, she and 20 Panther members were arrested.

They were dubbed the "Panther 21." Alice found herself pregnant and incarcerated in the Women's House of Detention in Greenwich Village. Alice represented herself in court, delivering, according to Connie Bruck in a July 1997 article in the *New Yorker*, "a withering cross-examination of a key prosecution witness, who turned out to be an undercover government agent." Fourteen of the original 21 co-defendants, including Alice, were acquitted in May 1971, only a month away from her delivery date.

On June 16, 1971, a son was born to Alice Williams. She and Garland parted ways soon after. Garland, who had two other children from previous relationships, saw his son off and on until he was five, then lost contact with him. Garland wouldn't see him again until 1992, after he saw Tupac's picture on a poster advertising the movie *Juice*.

The Las Vegas Metropolitan Police Department's homicide unit lists Tupac's given name as "Lesane Crooks." Lieutenant Larry Spinosa said the family gave officers that name. The Clark County Coroner shows the rapper's name as Tupac A. Shakur with an alias of Lesane Parish Crooks. It's not known where the surname Crooks came from.

Alice took the name Afeni Shakur after she married a man named Mutulu Shakur when Tupac was a toddler, and she gave her son the name Tupac Amaru after a warrior and the last Inca chief to be tortured and murdered by Spanish conquistadores. It means "Shining Serpent," which was an Incan symbol of wisdom and courage. Shakur is Arabic for "Thankful to God"; it's a common surname chosen by members of the Nation of Islam when they join the Muslim religion. Afeni never legally changed her son's name to Tupac Shakur, but that's what he went by the rest of his life.

Tupac was born a fighter.

"It's funny, because I never believed he would live," Afeni told writer Veronica Chambers about her son in an *Esquire* interview. "Every five years, I'd be just amazed that he made it to five, that he made it to ten, that he made it to fifteen. I had a million miscarriages, you know.

"This child stayed in my womb through the worst possible conditions. I had to get a court order to get an egg to eat every day. I had to get a court order to get a glass of milk every day—you know what I'm saying? I lost weight, but he gained weight. He was born one month and three days after we were acquitted. I had not been able to carry a child. This child comes and hangs on and really fights for his life."

After she was acquitted, Afeni went on the speakers circuit to talk about her experiences. But her celebrity was short-lived and Afeni found herself back on the welfare rolls, living in the ghetto.

Afeni settled with her baby boy in the Bronx. Two years later she gave birth to Tupac's half-sister, Sekyiwa Shakur. Sekyiwa's father, Mutulu, was also a Black Panther and a nationalist with the Nation of Islam. Mutulu called himself a doctor, claiming he received a degree in acupuncture in Canada.

In 1986, Mutulu was arrested and charged with masterminding a 1981 Brinks robbery in which two Nyack, New York, cops and a Brinks security guard were killed. Mutulu—born Jeral Wayne Williams—denied being involved in the hold-up. He was convicted anyway and is serving a 60-year sentence in a federal maximum-security penitentiary in Florence, Colorado. Mutulu was also convicted of conspiring to break Assata Shakur, Tupac's family friend, whom he called "aunt," out of prison. Assata was convicted in 1977 of murdering a New Jersey state trooper but escaped two years later and fled to Cuba. She remains at large.

Mutulu went underground after the Brinks holdup in 1981 and wasn't captured until 1986. He was on the FBI's Ten Most Wanted List until his capture. Tupac was taught early by Mutulu not to trust law-enforcement officers. FBI agents would periodically go to Tupac's school to ask him if he'd seen his stepdad. Mutulu, who was close to Tupac, kept in touch with him while he was on the run.

Tupac's godfather, Elmer "Geronimo" Pratt, a deputy minister in the Black Panther Party, also wasn't around when

Tupac was growing up. Pratt was sentenced to life in a California prison after his conviction for the murder of a white Los Angeles grammar school teacher when Tupac was an infant. Pratt's attorney at the time was a young Johnnie Cochran Jr., who would later go on to successfully defend former football star O.J. Simpson in the murder trial of Nicole Brown Simpson and Ronald Goldman. Pratt's case became, and remains, a famous civil-rights cause celebre for L.A.'s African-American community, because Cochran claimed racism. Cochran argued, and Pratt maintained throughout his incarceration, that Pratt was framed by law enforcement. After his conviction, Pratt was denied parole 16 times because he refused to renounce his politics or confess to the crime.

Geronimo Pratt walked out of prison in June 1997 after his conviction was overturned by an Orange County Superior Court judge, who declared that the Los Angeles County District Attorney's prosecution was unlawful and corrupt. His conviction was reversed on the grounds that the government suppressed evidence favorable to him at his trial, notably that the principal witness against him was a paid police informant. The decision was handed down midway through Pratt's 26th year in prison.

Tupac would later say he continued where Geronimo Pratt, Afeni and the Black Panthers, Mutulu Shakur, and Lumumba Shakur all left off. He referred to them in his lyrics as political prisoners.

Afeni and her children eventually moved to Harlem to live with Afeni's new lover, Legs, and in homeless shelters and with friends and relatives. But Legs, once linked to New York drug lord Nicky Barnes, was jailed for credit-card fraud, and died in prison at 41 from a crack-induced heart attack.

Legs, Tupac would later say, was the man who taught him about being a thug, an aspect of Legs' personality Tupac admired. He was also the only father he knew, and now he was gone. "I couldn't even cry, man," Tupac told writer Kevin Powell. "I felt I needed a daddy to show me the ropes, and I didn't have one."

When Tupac was 10 years old, a minister asked him what he wanted to be when he grew up, "A revolutionary," was his answer, because that was all he had ever known.

"Here we was, kickin' all this shit about the revolution and we starvin'," Tupac told Powell.

When Tupac was 12, something happened that changed his life. Afeni sent him to a Harlem theater group. He was a natural, and at 13 he played the role of Travis in "A Raisin in the Sun" at the famous Apollo Theatre for a Jesse Jackson fundraiser. Tupac liked performing on stage; through acting, he felt he could become someone worthy of respect. He might also have had an inkling back then that it could be a way to escape ghetto life.

In 1986 when Tupac was 15, Afeni moved her family to Baltimore, Maryland. There, Tupac entered the prestigious Baltimore High School for the Arts, after his mother talked the school into taking him. It marked another major turning point; this time it meant going to a school far removed from the ghetto. While at the school, he thrived, starring in several productions. He also started dabbling in rap. Besides music, Tupac studied ballet, poetry, and acting. It was at the Baltimore school that he began calling himself an artist. His classmates and teachers considered him talented. The "thug" in his personality hadn't emerged yet—at least he wasn't showing it.

Life at home, however, was still hand to mouth. Afeni often didn't have the money to pay her utility bills and the electricity in their apartment was shut off most of the time. Tupac, always the avid reader, studied outside by the light of the street lamps. He stayed at Baltimore High School for the Arts for two years. He told Kevin Powell, "That school was the freest I ever felt."

When a neighborhood boy was killed in a gang shooting during Tupac's junior year in 1988, Afeni put her kids on a Greyhound bus to spend the summer with a family friend who lived in Marin City, California. It turned out to be an area the cops called the "Jungle," a small ghetto just below pricey hillside homes across the bay from San Francisco in affluent Marin County. Afeni didn't realize she was simply sending her kids to another gang-infested ghetto, the same, or worse, than they'd lived in most of their lives. A few months later, after the friend called and said she was going into an alcohol rehabilitation center, Afeni moved to California, into low-income federal housing. The family lived in the heart of the Jungle, in Building 89, unit 1. Surrounded by neighborhood drug dealers, Afeni soon took on a cocaine habit.

Tupac, a skinny teenager, was taunted by the street drug dealers from whom his mother bought crack cocaine to feed her worsening habit.

"It'd be the shitty, dumb niggas who had women, rides, houses," he told Powell. "And I didn't have shit... They used to dis me..."

And to writer Veronica Chambers, Tupac said, "Everybody else's mother was just a regular mother, but my mother was Afeni—you know what I'm saying? My mother had a strong reputation. It was just like having a daddy because she had a rep. Motherfuckers get roasted if you fuck with Afeni or her children. Couldn't nobody touch us."

Still, Tupac felt he could no longer handle his mother's crack habit and moved out of her apartment and into an abandoned housing unit with a group of boys. They later formed the singing group One Nation Emcees. Even though he was a good student with a high grade-point average, Tupac eventually dropped out of high school at age 17 and worked odd jobs to survive, one at a pizza parlor. He also sold crack on the street to get by.

Tupac remembered crying a lot while he was growing up. Because his family moved around so much, often to homeless shelters, he never felt like he fit in anywhere. He led a lonely existence. He didn't have any long-term friends and felt pressured to reinvent himself each time his family moved to a new neighborhood. He felt vulnerable living in the ghetto. Kids made fun of him, calling him "Tuberculosis" and "Tube Sock" because of his name, and "Pretty" because of his good looks.

He told writer William Shaw he didn't have decent clothes and went to school "in the same things every day, holes in my jeans, the fucked-up sneakers. You don't want to be Tupac. You want to be *Jack*."

It was in the Bay Area that Tupac got into hip-hop music. He started writing poetry, then turned his poems into songs. He called himself MC New York. When he wasn't writing lyrics, Tupac spent his spare time reading. He couldn't get enough of books, movies, and music. He was hungry for knowledge.

It was here that he came into his own with his rap style— where he rhymed straight and to the point, where his lyrics became direct, where he learned not to pretend to be someone or something he wasn't. His family was still poor, still living in the ghetto, but he admitted it and wasn't ashamed of it—keepin' it real, as he would often say.

In 1986, Tupac and his friends in the Jungle formed a rap group and named it Two From the Crew. They wrote songs, including "Lifestyles of the Poor and Homeless," "Let's Get It On," and "Get Ourselves the Girls." But their theme song was called "Thug Life," so named because people in the neighborhood referred to the teenagers as young thugs. Tupac said his music showed how he and others like him lived. The lyrics about violence involving police, for example, were based on actual stories of what young black men faced in the ghetto. The thug-life image for which he would later become famous was born.

"You were just givin' truth to the music," Tupac later told San Francisco's KMEL deejay Sway. "Being in Marin City was like a small town, so it taught me to be more straightforward with my style. Instead of being so metaphorical with the rhyme, I was encouraged to go straight at it and hit it dead on and not waste time trying to cover things. In Marin City, everything was straightforward. Poverty was straightforward. There was no way to say 'I'm poor' but to say 'I'm poor.'"

He wouldn't be poor much longer.

• • •

While Tupac's friends in the Jungle rapped with him for the fun of it, they later said that rap became Tupac's obsession, even as a teenager. Tupac got his foot in the door of the professional music world when he met Leila Steinberg, a young white woman, at a San Francisco park. They became fast friends and Tupac made her his manager. Leila, a part-time teacher at Bayside Elementary, a school near the Jungle, got Tupac involved in poetry readings. Also a show promoter, Leila was already working with a rapper named Ray Love. She introduced Tupac to Love and the two began rapping together as the group Strictly Dope. Tupac moved into Leila's house in Sonoma County and his public life began.

Leila introduced him to Atron Gregory, the manager of the Grammy-nominated Digital Underground, a seminal Bay Area rap ensemble. One of the things that attracted Atron to Tupac was that Tupac's lyrics and rhymes were straight from the street. It was what Tupac called "keeping it real, keeping it street."

Tupac started out in 1989 at the age of 18 as a roadie and tour dancer and worked his way up to rapper, debuting on the "Sons of The P." album. Tupac was a "humpty-hump" dancer on stage, performing while the singers, including Queen Latifah and Shock G, rapped. Shock G started allowing Tupac to rap on stage and eventually on an album. Tupac continued rapping with Digital Underground under his moniker, MC New York, and went on a world tour with the group.

After the tour, Tupac rented his own apartment in Oakland. He'd earned enough money to buy a lime-green Toyota Celica. He also spent some money on firearms. His friends went over to his apartment to "kick it," listen to Tupac's music, smoke blunts, and play with his new guns, which included 12 gauges, a Glock 9, and an AK-47. He felt he was on his way up. He had the possessions to prove it. But he still went back to the Jungle regularly to visit his friends, proudly driving through the projects in his bright green car.

Soon, he'd recorded enough songs for a solo album, but he couldn't get a record company to release it. One of the labels that rejected him was Tommy Boy Records.

"He was funny, adorable, a real flirt," Tommy Boy Records president Monica Lynch told William Shaw for an article in *Vanity Fair*. "But as an artist, he wasn't there."

By this time, 1990, gangsta was in style, hot, especially in Los Angeles. Dr. Dre was there, Snoop Doggy Dogg, Eazy-E, and the Ices'—T and Cube. Gangsta was popular with young whites as well as blacks.

While waiting for a record deal, Tupac went with his friend Money-B to an audition for a movie called *Juice*, a coming-of-age drama. Money-B was trying out for the part of a punk named Bishop, but he didn't do well. Tupac asked to audition. The producer, Neil Moritz, agreed to let him read. He was "dynamic, bold, powerful, magnetic—any word you want to use," Moritz said later. "Tupac was it. We cast him right on the spot." They shot Tupac's part in Harlem with Spike Lee's cinematographer, Ernest Dickerson, directing. Moritz congratulated Tupac after his performance and told him, "Ten years from now, you're going to be a big star."

"Ten years from now," Tupac responded, "I'm not going to be alive."

Juice marked another turning point in Tupac's life. Now he was not only a rap star, but a movie star. In interviews for a video biography of Tupac, *Thug Immortal*, his friends claimed that before he made the movie, he had a softer side to him. But while playing the role of Bishop, a street-smart hard-core thug, it was as if Tupac decided to *become* the character. He took on the persona of Bishop and began talking and acting tough. His friends said he wasn't really like that, he was just trying to look hard, because he thought it was expected of him as a thug rapper. His friends later described him as a "chameleon," becoming whatever he thought those around him wanted him to become. About that time, Tupac had "Thug Life" tattooed across his midriff.

But Tupac later claimed that Bishop was just a reflection of one type of young black male today; he said that all young black males weren't violent. The role of Lucky, which he played in the movie *Poetic Justice*, was just the opposite, that of a young black man who was a parent, lived at home, and was working to get ahead.

Atron Gregory, in the meantime, was trying to set up a deal with Interscope Records, an independent label owned by department-store heir Ted Field (heir to the Marshall Field fortune) and Jimmy Iovine, a former John Lennon record producer. At the time, Interscope was in a partnership with Warner Music Group, a subsidiary of Time Warner. Interscope president Tom Whalley signed Tupac to Interscope. Interscope and Gregory sealed a deal for Tupac's debut album, *2pacalypse Now*. Released in 1992, it went on to sell $90 million worth.

"Right away you could tell that this guy [Tupac] was different from the rest of the world," Tom Whalley told *Vanity Fair's* William Shaw. "I couldn't slow him down. I never worked with anyone who could write so many great songs so quickly."

Tupac's rap had a fresh voice, a fresh style, on the gangsta scene. There was a softness behind his bad-boy persona. He had an emotional depth that was revealed in the more contemplative lyrics in his music. But beneath the surface, he was an angry young man, haunted by demons from his youth that surfaced in his lyrics.

He demonstrated his unique range as a performer on *2pacalypse Now*. The record included militant lyrics depicting violence between young black men and the police, drawing on the gang culture of South Central Los Angeles. The hit single "Brenda's Got A Baby," with its references to cops being killed, caused an uproar. Then-Vice President Dan Quayle singled out the album, criticizing it for its encouragement of violence, cop killing, and its disrespect for women. Quayle, in his war against the breakdown of traditional values in the entertainment industry, used Tupac as an example, saying that Tupac's lyrics had "no place in our society." Bolstered by the invaluable publicity, the CD catapulted Tupac's career into star territory. He was nominated that year for an "American Music Award" as best new rap hip-hop artist.

In the video biography, *Thug Immortal*, writer Tony Patrick described Tupac as charismatic.

"There was something special about him," Patrick said. "You saw it in his records. I saw it a little bit more in his movies. He had that glow. He had that charisma. There was no one else who looked like him. He had the eyebrows. He had the cheekbones. You know, handsome. Sometimes when you saw him sitting there introspective, if you were a woman you wanted to go over there and ask him, 'Pac, what's wrong? What can I do for you, baby?' He had that special glow about him that attracted you to him right away."

While *2pacalypse Now* was still on the charts, Tupac's film debut in *Juice* hit screens around the country.

Juice Director Ernest Dickerson spoke to MTV about what it was like directing the rap star. He described Tupac as a thinking man.

"I think that he's very introspective," Dickerson said. "I mean, when we were shooting *Juice*, in between takes he would spend a lot of time by himself, writing. You know, he thinks a lot. He thinks about what's going on in the world, he thinks about what's going on in the neighborhoods, and he talks about it in his music. The thing that I really got from Tupac was that he was always thinking, always at work. His mind was always going."

In early 1992, after the filming of *Juice* wrapped up, Tupac and long-time friend Charles "Man-Man" Fuller moved from northern California to South Central Los Angeles. Tupac began taking target practice at shooting ranges and working out with weights. His success continued to soar.

Tupac's critical acclaim for *Juice* led to his second movie role, co-starring as Lucky opposite Janet Jackson in *Poetic Justice*. *Poetic Justice* director John Singleton also praised Tupac's acting abilities. Singleton told *Vibe* magazine, "He's what they call a natural. You know, he's a real actor. He has all these methods and everything, philosophies about how a role should be played. (*Vibe* magazine has published a collection of interviews with Tupac in a book, *Tupac Shakur by the Editors of Vibe Magazine*.)

"When I saw *Juice*, Tupac's performance jumped out at me like a tiger. Here was an actor who could portray the ultimate crazy nigga. A brother who could embody the freedom that an 'I don't give a fuck' mentality gives a black man. I thought, 'This was some serious acting.' Maybe I was wrong.

"During the filming of *Poetic Justice*, 'Pac both rebelled and accepted my attitude toward him as a director [and] advisor. This was our dance in life and work. We'd argue, then make up. Tupac spoke from a position that cannot be totally appreciated unless you understood the pathos of being a nigga, a displaced African soul, full of power, pain, and passion, with no focus or direction for all that energy except his art."

Writer Veronica Chambers was on the set of *Poetic Justice* at the invitation of Singleton, who wanted her to author a behind-the-scenes book. In an *Esquire* article after Tupac's death, she reported that "Tupac had a hard time following the rules.

"Half the time, there were no problems at all," she wrote, "but it wasn't unusual for Tupac to get high in his trailer, to be hours late to the set in the morning, or to get pissed off for what seemed like no reason at all. Once, toward the end of the shoot, Tupac was told he could have a day off. That morning, the producers decided that they would shoot publicity stills and called Tupac to the set. He arrived with his homeboys and began screaming, 'I can't take this shit. Y'all treat a nigga like a slave.' He stormed off to his trailer and promptly punched in a window.

"It certainly wasn't the first time a star has had a fit on a set. But Tupac was a young black male with more than a little street credibility. At the time, nobody knew how far he was willing to take his mantras about living a 'thug life.' There was indignation on the set about being blasted by some young punk, but there was also fear: fear both *of* Tupac and *for* Tupac. I believe this was a pattern of concern that those around him felt right up until his death."

In late 1993, Tupac, his step brother Mopreme (aka Maurice Harding), and three others recorded *Thug Life, Volume I*. Although it was hard-core rap, the album went gold.

Tupac had escaped from the ghetto, but he couldn't seem to get the ghetto out of his blood. As he experienced first-hand the tough gangsta life he rapped about, his own rap sheet grew. Starting in 1992, when Tupac was charged with battery for slapping a woman who asked for his autograph, criminal charges and civil lawsuits loomed over him like a dark cloud. At one point, Tupac was scheduled for court dates in Los Angeles, Atlanta, New York, and Detroit, all within a two-week period. He was doing his part to live up to the bad-boy image he'd cultivated for himself.

Mopreme has said that when Tupac's second solo album with Interscope, *Strictly 4 My N.I.G.G.A.Z.*, was released in 1994 with a red cover, everyone thought Tupac had become a member of the Bloods gang. While he sometimes hung out with Bloods, he also, on occasion, hung out with Crips. But Tupac came to be more identified with the Bloods, especially after he signed on with Death Row Records, run by Suge Knight, whose connection to the Bloods ran deep. Tupac's affiliation may have come back to haunt him in his beef at the MGM Grand with Orlando Anderson, who is said to be a member of the rival Crips gang.

In 1992, Tupac was involved in a civil wrongful-death lawsuit after a six-year-old boy was killed at a northern California festival celebrating the 50th anniversary of the Marin City neighborhood, the Jungle, where Tupac had lived as a teenager. The boy was caught in gunfire between a member of Tupac's crew and a rival gang member. Interscope Records, under which Tupac recorded at the time, settled with the boy's family out of court for nearly a half million dollars. Tupac was never charged with a crime.

On April 5, 1993, Tupac was arrested and accused of trying to hit a fellow rapper with a baseball bat at a concert at Michigan State University. The incident was apparently triggered when Tupac got angry over something, then threw a $670 microphone that belonged to the group MAD. Rapper Chauncey Wynn publicly objected to Tupac's behavior. A near-riot broke out when the audience stormed the entertainers; security guards and police had to clear more than 3,000 people from around the stage.

Tupac testified he'd been clutching the baseball bat, which he said he used as a prop at the concert. He told the court he didn't hit or attempt to hit anyone and that the bat had scared the other rapper.

Tupac, 23 at the time, pleaded guilty on September 14, 1994, to a misdemeanor in exchange for prosecutors dropping felony assault charges. He returned for sentencing on October 26. He could have gotten up to 90 days in the East Lansing jail. Instead, he was sentenced to, and served, 10 days in jail, and ordered to perform 35 hours of community service.

It would only get worse.

During a 1993 concert at a Pine Bluff, Arkansas, nightclub, a woman named Jacquelyn McNealey was hit by a stray bullet. The bullet damaged her spinal cord, leaving her paralyzed below the chest. After Tupac's death, she sued the nightclub and Tupac's estate, claiming Tupac "was taunting the crowd. He created a riot-like atmosphere which ended up in a shooting," her lawyer argued. The judge granted full damages of $16.6 million after Tupac's representatives failed to appear at the hearing. Richard Fischbein, attorney for Tupac's mother and his estate, told The Associated Press he had not been notified of the lawsuit nor of the judgment. The nightclub settled for $500,000. The gunman was prosecuted and sent to prison.

On October 31, 1993, Tupac was charged in the shooting of two off-duty police officers in Atlanta. Witnesses testified that Tupac and his associates shot back at the plainclothes officers after they fired at Tupac's car. The charges were eventually dropped when it was learned that the cops, who'd been drinking, had initiated the incident, and when the prosecution's own witness testified that the gun used by an officer to threaten Tupac had earlier been seized in a drug bust and was missing from a police evidence locker.

Tupac also served some time for an altercation on the set of a music video. The fight involved Tupac and the video's directors, Albert and Allen Hughes. The brothers had fired Tupac from the cast of *Menace II Society* six months earlier because of his violent temper.

Tupac told his side of the story to *Vibe* magazine. "[The Hughes brothers] was doin' all my videos," he said. "After I did *Juice*, they said, 'Can we use your name to get this movie deal? I said, 'Hell, yeah.' When I got with John Singleton, he told me he wanted to be 'Scorsese to your DeNiro. For starring roles I just want you to work with me.' So I told the Hughes brothers I only wanted a little role. But I didn't tell them I wanted a sucker role. We was arguing about that in rehearsal. They said to me, 'Ever since you got with John Singleton's shit you changed.' They was trippin' 'cuz they got this thing with John Singleton. They feel like they competing with him."

A few months after the firing, Tupac ran into the Hughes brothers at a video taping. The three argued. Tupac told *Vibe*, "That's a fair fight, am I right? Two niggas against me?"

Tupac was charged with carrying a loaded concealed weapon. He faced the possibility of a year in jail and a $3,000 fine. He was convicted of misdemeanor assault and battery on February 10, 1994, and sentenced in March to 15 days in Los Angeles County Jail and 15 days on a California Department of Transportation road crew, which he reluctantly served. He later said he hated being jailed, which made him feel smothered. Rumors that he was raped by fellow inmates were never substantiated. His friends claim it never happened.

Tupac's most notorious criminal rap came when he was accused of sexually abusing a female fan. The woman alleged that Tupac and two pals held her down while a fourth man sodomized her in a hotel room.

Tupac had begun hanging out with a Haitian-born music promoter named Jacques Agnant. On the night of November 14, 1993, Agnant took Tupac to Nell's, a downtown New York nightclub, and introduced him to a 19-year-old Manhattan woman named Ayanna Jackson. Jackson performed oral sex on Tupac on the dance floor, and they had more sex later that night in his hotel room.

Jackson returned to Tupac's hotel room at the Parker Meridien, a posh Manhattan hotel, four days later to collect her belongings. The two ended up in the bedroom. She said that as she and Tupac were kissing, three men burst into the room, and that Tupac and the men stripped off her underwear, then sodomized and sexually abused her. After she left the hotel, she filed a police report accusing the four of gang raping her.

Jackson testified that Jacques Agnant and a friend of his, along with Charles Fuller and Tupac, were in the room when she was gang raped. Tupac, Agnant, and Fuller were arrested and charged with sexual assault. Agnant's friend had left the room earlier (and wasn't charged with a crime). A prosecutor told the court that Tupac liked the woman so much, "he decided to share her as a reward for his boys."

All three beat the rape charge. Agnant copped a plea to a misdemeanor, while Tupac and Fuller were convicted of three counts of first-degree sexual abuse, which means they groped and touched the victim without her consent. Tupac and Fuller were sentenced to two-and-a-half years in prison. They were cleared of sodomy charges, which, if they'd been convicted, required a prison term of up to 25 years. A jury rejected the woman's claim that Tupac forced group sex on her and convicted the rapper of the lesser sex-abuse charge. Tupac, at 22 years of age, was sent to the Clinton Correctional Facility in

Dannemora, New York. Considering he wasn't convicted of rape, Tupac's attorneys and associates were stunned that he was sent to the maximum-security prison.

Meanwhile, in a highly unconventional ruling, a judge agreed to sever Jacques Agnant's case from Tupac's and Charles Fuller's case. Tupac later became convinced that Agnant was a government informer and had set him up.

Tupac and Fuller were also acquitted of weapons charges; police had found two unlicensed handguns in the men's hotel suite. Tupac's lawyer, Michael Warren, successfully argued that the weapons didn't belong to the pair.

The verdict came a day after Tupac was shot five times while resisting an apparent robbery. He was being treated at a hospital when the verdict was to be read, and insisted that he be released from the hospital so he could face the jury. He wanted them to look him in the eye as they read the verdict. He went in a wheelchair, but had to leave early because he felt too sick.

For all his legal notoriety, it was that first shooting that was Tupac's most famous incident. On November 30, 1994, Tupac was gunned down in the lobby of Quad Studios, a Manhattan recording studio in Times Square, assaulted by men police described as robbers.

Tupac, who was in Manhattan for the verdict in the sexual assault case, had been invited by Ron G., a deejay in New York, to record with him. Tupac agreed to do the recording for free, as a favor to the young rapper, whom he wanted to help out. (He usually charged other rappers a fee to record on their albums.) After finishing the taping session, Tupac was paged by a rapper named Booker, who asked him to tape a song with Little Shawn, an East Coast rapper.

Tupac told him he'd do it that day, for $7,000. Booker agreed, and told him to go to Quad Studios in Manhattan. While heading out to the studio, Tupac got a second call from Booker asking why he was taking so long. Then came a third call telling Tupac they didn't have the money to pay. Tupac told Booker he wouldn't record unless he was paid, and hung up. Finally, he got a fourth call from Booker telling him that Uptown Entertainment would take care of the money, which would be waiting for him when he was finished recording. Tupac said he was on his way to the studio. By that time, it was midnight.

Tupac, his half-sister Sekyiwa, her boyfriend Zayd, rapper Randy "Stretch" Walker, and a friend identified only as Fred entered the lobby of Quad Studios. Tupac wasn't worried about entering the building late at night; he didn't expect trouble and he was armed. The attack took him totally by surprise.

The group noticed two men wearing Army fatigues, recognized by Tupac as gang garb worn mostly in the Brooklyn area; a third gang-related man was already in the lobby, pretending to read a newspaper. As the group waited at the elevator, the two fatigues-clad men, carrying identical handguns, approached them. They went straight for Tupac, ordering him to the floor and demanding he give up all his jewelry and money. When Tupac went for his own gun stashed in his waistband, they shot him. A round hit him in the groin area and passed through his thigh. That bullet cost him a testicle. Then the gunmen began beating him. They ripped his jewelry off him, then shot him again, hitting him in the chest. Altogether he was shot five times: in his head, chest, thigh, groin, and left arm. No one else was attacked. Only Tupac.

Two years later, in one of the last interviews he'd give to *Vibe* magazine, Tupac spoke to a reporter about what it felt like to get shot.

"...The dude with the newspaper was holding the gun on (Stretch). He was telling the light-skinned dude, 'Shoot that motherfucker! Fuck it!' Then I got scared, because the dude had the gun to my stomach. All I could think about was piss bags and shit bags.

"I drew my arm around him to move the gun to my side. He shot and the gun twisted and that's when I got hit the first time. I felt it in my leg; I didn't know I got shot in my balls. I dropped to the floor. Everything in my mind said, 'Pac, pretend you're dead.' It didn't matter. They started kicking me, hitting me. I never said, 'Don't shoot!' I was quiet as hell. They were snatchin' my shit off me while I was laying on the floor. I had my eyes closed, but I was shaking, because the situation had me shaking. And then I felt something in the back of my head, something real strong. I thought they stomped me or pistol-whipped me, and they were stomping my head against the concrete. I saw white, just white. I didn't hear nothin'. I didn't feel nothin', and I said, 'I'm unconscious.' But I was conscious.

"And then I felt it again, and I could hear things now and I could see things and they were bringing me back to consciousness. Then they did it again, and I couldn't hear nothin'. And I couldn't see nothing; it was just all white. And then they hit me again, and I could hear things and I could see things and I knew I was conscious again."

After the attack, Tupac was helped up by Fred and Stretch. He was passing out. They started to walk to the front door and saw police coming. So they headed for the elevator and went up to the studio where Biggie Smalls was supposed to be recording. Once upstairs, Tupac, bleeding from his wounds, managed to call his girlfriend. He told her to phone his mother and tell her he'd been shot. Tupac also tried to talk to Biggie and Sean "Puffy" Combs, CEO of Bad Boy Entertainment, Biggie's rap label, whom he later suspected of setting him up.

Meanwhile, someone called paramedics and Tupac was taken by ambulance to a nearby hospital. As paramedics were lifting him into the ambulance, Tupac flipped off a newspaper photographer, who caught the gesture on film. Though he was shot five times, the prognosis was good: he would live. He checked out of the hospital shortly after his surgery the next day, because he thought the gunmen might show up to finish the job. He recovered at the New York home of a friend, actress Jasmine Guy.

Jacques Agnant, the Haitian music promoter who introduced Tupac to the woman who accused him of rape, also had ties to Little Shawn (who asked Tupac to rap with him in Quad Studios). Tupac later rapped about Agnant in his album *The Don Killuminati:* "About a snitch named Haitian Jack, Knew he was working for the feds... Set me up." Agnant has filed a libel suit against Tupac's estate, Death Row, Interscope, the producer and engineer of the song, and the publishing company.

The New York Police Department's investigation of the Quad Studios shooting ended shortly after it began, due, the cops claimed, to lack of cooperation on Tupac's part. But what the New York cops considered to be a break in the case came in October 1996, about a month after Tupac was killed in Las Vegas.

In a published statement, federal prosecutors in New York said that Walter Johnson, aka "King Tut," a 17-year career criminal, was a suspect in the 1994 shooting. Johnson was jailed in October 1996 and charged with twelve federal felony counts stemming from three armed robberies in Brooklyn. The charges didn't include Tupac's shooting, though law enforcement sources told the *New York Daily News* that they were investigating statements he allegedly made to a confidential informant. "He (Johnson) said Tupac is a sucker," the informant told investigators. "He said Tupac is not a real gangster and that he shot him." As of July 1997, Johnson had not been charged.

Investigators also told the newspaper the Johnson investigation could help solve Tupac's slaying. "We hope this will lead to a solution of the murder of Tupac," one source close to the investigation told the *Daily News*.

Metro's Sergeant Manning didn't remember talking to New York City police about the case, adding, "The only King Tut I've heard of is the one in Egypt."

Manning did say he'd spoken a few times to N.Y.P.D. detectives, but just briefly, about the Manhattan shooting.

While Tupac was recuperating from the attack in a New York hospital, Billy Garland, Tupac's real father, visited him. Garland told writer Kevin Powell, "I had to be there. He's

A young Tupac, in the days of stogies (blunts), forty-
ouncers, bandanas, non-designer underwear, and less-
defined abdominal muscles. (Trilobite)

Good times—Tupac partying after the 1995 Soul Train
Awards ceremony. (Trilobite)

Bad times—Being led
to jail by N.Y.P.D. officers after being arrested
for sexual abuse in
Manhattan. Tupac later
said, "Before I made a
record, I never had a
record." (AP/Wide
World Photos)

Suge Knight arrives at the hospital after Tupac's death to pay his respects to Afeni Shakur. (R. Marsh Starks/*Las Vegas Sun*)

Mug shot of Suge taken earlier the same day when he registered in Las Vegas as an ex-felon.

Bad Boy Entertainment's rapper Biggie Smalls (left) and CEO Puffy Combs on the set of one of the last videos they shot together. (Trilobite)

The scuffle at MGM Grand. From top: a frame from the video surveillance tape of the attack in the casino; minutes later, Tupac storms toward the MGM entrance; Orlando Anderson is later identified as the beating victim.

Aerial photo of the BMW's course. (1) The shooting occurred at the intersection of Koval Lane and E. Flamingo Rd. Suge made a U-turn and headed west on Flamingo, to (2) the corner of Flamingo and Las Vegas Blvd., where he clipped the median making a left turn onto the Strip. At point (3), the intersection of Harmon Avenue and the Strip, the BMW finally came to a stop. (Jason Cox)

Club 662, where Suge and Tupac were headed, is located two miles farther east on Flamingo. (AP/ Wide World Photos)

Members of Tupac's entourage wait to be questioned by homicide detectives at the corner where the BMW came to rest. (Malcolm Payne)

Homicide Sergeant Kevin Manning presides over the only news conference about the investigation conducted by Las Vegas police. (Steve Marcus/*Las Vegas Sun*)

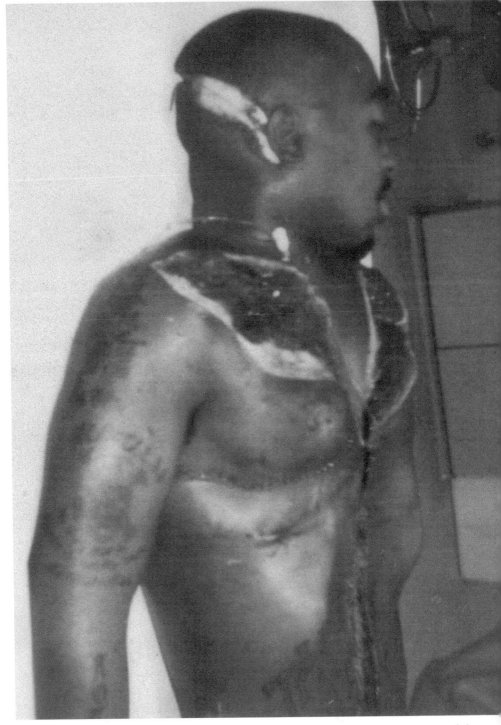

The photo—Tupac Shakur on the coroner's autopsy table.

my son. I've never asked him for anything—not money or nothing. I just wanted to let him know that I cared. He thought I was dead or that I didn't want to see him. How could I feel like that? He's my flesh and blood. Look at me. He looks just like me. People who I had never seen before immediately knew I was his father."

Tupac did 11 months of hard time at Clinton Correctional before being bailed out pending an appeal for the sexual abuse conviction. While in incarcerated, he married his girlfriend, Keisha Morris, a student he'd dated for six months before being jailed. The marriage was annulled shortly after Tupac was released. Tupac later said it was a marriage of convenience and seemed right while he was in prison. But once he was released, his busy career and fast lifestyle got in the way of the relationship. He and Keisha parted as friends.

While in prison, Tupac continually told his friends that he needed to get out. If he did, he vowed he wouldn't return to the thug lifestyle. He claimed he would turn over a new leaf. Death Row Records' Suge Knight and his attorney, David Kenner, visited Tupac at the New York prison. Tupac told Suge, "I want to join the family. Just get me out." Suge and Kenner, apparently trying to capitalize on Tupac's desperation, presented him with a four-page hand-written recording contract that committed Tupac to three albums for the Death Row "family." In return? Suge and Kenner would get Tupac out of prison by posting the $1.4 million bond required for him to be released during the appeals process. Tupac signed. He also agreed to appoint Kenner, Death Row's long-time attorney, as his own lawyer.

Some said it was only because Tupac was in prison that he signed the contract with Death Row. Tupac was the bread-winner for his family—cousins, niece, mother, and sister. He had attorney fees and other lawsuits to settle. Death Row bailed him out, and not just out of jail, but financially, as well.

Friends and associates warned Tupac that he'd be selling his soul, that he'd be owned by Suge and Death Row, but Tupac signed on the dotted line.

"Why they let me go, I don't know, but I'm out," Tupac rapped in a music video after his release.

Tupac was a free man. He was grateful to be free. Waiting for him upon his release was a private chartered jet that flew him from New York to Los Angeles. That same night, he was in an L.A. studio recording an album for the Death Row label. Within three days after his release from prison, he'd recorded seven songs. They marked the beginning of a torrent of songs—some 200 of them—Tupac would record between then and his fatal shooting a year later.

"There's nobody in the business strong enough to scare me," Tupac said during a *Vibe* magazine interview. "I'm with Death Row 'cause they not scared either." Tupac was openly grateful to Suge.

"When I was in jail, Suge was the only one who used to see me. Nigga used to fly a private plane all the way to New York and spend time with me. He got his lawyer to look into all my cases. Suge supported me, whatever I needed. When I got out of jail, he had a private plane for me, a limo, five police officers for security. I said, 'I need a house for my moms.' I got a house for my moms.

"I promised him, 'Suge, I'm gonna make Death Row the biggest label in the whole world. I'm gonna make it bigger than Snoop ever made it.' Not stepping on Snoop's toes; he did a lot of work—him, Dogg Pound, Nate Dogg, Dre, all of them—they made Death Row what it is today. I'm gonna take it to the next level."

Tupac's Death Row Records solo debut, the double-CD *All Eyez on Me*, sold $14 million in its first week in stores. It was the fastest-selling CD of 1996. Containing 27 songs with titles such as "Shorty Wanna Be a Thug," "Wonda Why They

Call U Bytch," and "Ratha Be Ya Nigga," *All Eyez on Me* sold seven million copies.

Death Row was the premier rap label, producing more platinum albums than any other label. And it wasn't just black youths from the ghetto who were buying the record. White boys from middle America were also lining up to hear his sound. The majority of fans and buyers of rap music are middle-class white youths; 70% of those who buy rap music are white. Not everyone, however, understood why so many were drawn to Tupac's music.

Richard Roeper, a columnist for the *Chicago Sun-Times*, called Tupac "a street-talking clown obsessed with guns, money, sex, and killing.

"His success isn't the story of someone rising above the thug life through his talent. It's the story of someone wallowing in it," wrote Roeper.

"As I write this," he continued, "I'm listening to *All Eyez On Me*. If I hear the words 'motherfucker,' 'bitch' or 'nigger' one more time, I'm going to open the window and throw my little stereo into the sea. There's scarcely a mention of the word 'love' in any of the more than two dozen songs, but the aforementioned words appear more than 100 times apiece. It's a soundtrack for the '90s. Meet Tupac Shakur."

Tupac called Kevin Powell to the state prison while he was incarcerated. As he smoked one cigarette after another, he told the reporter from *Vibe* magazine, "This is my last interview. If I get killed, I want people to get every drop. I want them to have the real story."

Tupac told Powell that when he was first incarcerated, fellow inmates said of him, "Fuck that gangsta rapper." He was insulted. He didn't like being recognized only as a gangsta rapper; he considered himself a full-fledged rapper, one who was paving the way for others to follow. He said he rapped about life, which included a lot of violence. He considered himself saddled with more responsibilities than others his age, because people looked up to him, turned to him for answers. But there was a major problem: he'd been smoking so much marijuana and drinking so much alcohol that he was barely coherent. He called himself a weed addict. Then he went to jail and was forced to get clean. Once off pot and booze, his mind began to clear. He talked to Powell about two of his favorite themes: race and black-on-black violence.

"The real tragedy is that there are some ignorant brothers out here," Tupac told Powell. "That's why I'm not on this all-white or all-black shit. I'm on this all-real or all-fake shit with people, whatever color you are. Because niggas will do you. I mean, there's some foul niggas out there. The same niggas that did Malcolm X. The same niggas that did Jesus Christ. Every brother ain't a brother. They will do you. So just because it's black don't mean it's cool. And just because it's white don't mean it's evil."

Upon his release from prison, Tupac renounced the thug life (an acronym for The Hate U Give Little Infants Fucks Everybody), but his ambition for his career and passion for music were untamed. He was trying to keep the two elements of his career—movie and music—on track. He was also appealing his conviction for sexual abuse.

Tupac and Suge were inseparable in the months after Tupac's release from prison. In between recording sessions, Suge took Tupac to Mexico and Hawaii. In return, Tupac brought a fresh star image, a charisma, to Death Row that the other rappers didn't have.

He claimed that he was rehabilitated. He used his performance in the movie *Gridlock'd* to prove it. "If nothing else," he said about his work on the film, "it'll just prove that I can show up to the set on time and still have an album that sells five million while I'm doing my shit. It'll just show that I work hard. Also, it'll show that I should not be in jail 'cause in the little bit of time I've been out, I've showed that I can be rehabilitated out here with everybody else. It's the money that rehabilitates me, not the jail." Tupac wanted people to know that he worked hard, that he wasn't a slouch.

But, as the world would later learn, Tupac was far from rehabilitated. He got out of prison swearing he was a changed man, but he quickly succumbed to the same gangsta lifestyle. Maybe worse.

Tupac became Death Row's artistic centerpiece, its biggest star. And Death Row became the biggest rap label.

In 1995, following the multi-million-dollar success of his CD *Me Against The World* (with Interscope), and his co-starring role, with Mickey Rourke, in *Bullet,* Tupac founded a company, Euphanasia, to manage his film and music careers. Euphanasia was listed as his employer on the Clark County Coroner's report of his death. Months after his death, the business was still operating. Seven months later, however, the telephone number had been disconnected and the office at 8489 West Third Street, Suite 1038, in Los Angeles was closed.

A few months before his death, Tupac had become engaged to Quincy Jones' daughter, Kidada Jones. He had known her for just a few months. Tupac once publicly criticized Quincy Jones for marrying Kidada's mother, a white woman and former "Mod Squad" star, Peggy Lipton. Kidada, who met Tupac at a nightclub, reportedly took a while to warm up to him because of that. After dating a short time, they moved together into a Calabasas estate leased by Death Row. Tupac installed banks of video games and slot machines in a game room for his friends and relatives who often stayed with the couple at their house.

Tupac's feelings about women were complex and contradictory. In a 1995 interview on MTV, he said his songs attacked loose women, but not all women. He told journalist Tony Patrick, "There ain't nothin' like a black woman." (He also rapped about his allegiance to his other "girlfriend," his favorite pistol.)

His feelings about children were, however, simple. In an *Esquire* article, Tupac talked about why he didn't want to have any.

"Procreation is so much about ego," he said. "Everybody wants to have a junior. But I could care less about having a junior to tell, 'I got fucked by America and you're about to get fucked too.' Until we get a world where I feel like a first-class citizen, I can't have a child. 'Cause my child has to be a first-class citizen, and I'm not having no white babies.

"There's no way around it unless I want to turn white, turn my back on what's really going on in America. I either will be in jail or dead or be so fuckin' stressed out from not going to jail or dying or being on crack that I'd just pop a vessel. I'll just die from a heart attack. All the deaths are not going to be from the police killing you."

During the last year of his life, Tupac's acting career was skyrocketing. Vondie Curtis Hall, star of TV's "Chicago Hope," directed Tupac in the film *Gridlock'd*—which opened nationwide on January 29, 1997—a dark comedy about survival adapted from Hall's semi-autobiographical screenplay. He told *Parade* magazine that Tupac wasn't difficult to direct, despite his reputation to the contrary.

"When we cast Tupac, he'd just gotten out of jail, and a lot of people were leery of working with him. But he never caused problems," Hall insisted, "always coming to work prepared and on time. We never sensed that his luck was running out."

At the 1997 Sundance Film Festival four months after Tupac was killed, actor Tim Roth talked about starring opposite the rapper in *Gridlock'd*.

"It was great [working with him]," Roth told a reporter for the *Park Record* in Park City, Utah. "I know him only from the set, so I didn't know his music and I hadn't seen his films, and he preferred that. When he came to meet me for the first time, he said, 'Please don't see any [films] if you haven't. Don't listen to the music. Don't see the videos. People are going to tell you things, and some of them are going to be true and some of them aren't, but try to come with a clean slate.'

"He was very charming, very witty. He's a good actor, I think. My experience with him, we spent a lot of time laughing. I mean, we would get pissed off at each other and that's the normal way of things day to day, but we had a good time. A lot of stuff came out in the press, almost as though he deserved it when he died, but I look at him and I think, 'Wow, that's a great actor.' If I saw the film and wasn't in it, just saw it, I would think, 'I would love to work with that guy.' So it is tragic. He was constantly writing. He would film during the day, then go off and direct videos, or produce videos, or be in the studio recording music or go off and write music. He was prolific."

Tupac played the straight man to Roth's crazy-junkie character.

"Comedy only works when you have somebody good and solid to fire your stuff off of," Roth told the *Park Record*. "Although Tupac was really funny in the film, he makes a really good straight man."

In an interview with *Mr. Showbiz* magazine, Roth said Tupac had a work ethic that surpassed others he worked with. "He worked harder than any of us. He would be off directing videos at night and then go into the studio until four or five in the morning. Then he would be very tired and he would sleep as often as he could when there was down time. But he was very professional..."

"He talked about dying a lot," Roth told *Mr. Showbiz*, "because he knew it would happen. He knew he wasn't going to live to a ripe old age. It just was not going to be what happened to him... He really wanted to get away from what was expected from him, from how people had pigeonholed him, and move on and do different things. That's why he was doing *Gridlock'd*. It was part of that change—which is a very adult emotion, so he was somebody who was really growing. He had all the talent to do that, and he had the power and the money to do that. But on the other hand, he couldn't keep his mouth shut. We'd talk about that, how exhausting it is to be that testosterone guy they want you to be on the street, then I would see an interview with him and he would talk about his life in a very mature way, and then I would see another interview with him and he would be getting in somebody's face. Like everybody, he had a very childish aspect and a very mature aspect. And they were in conflict. He knew there was no clear-cut way out of where he was at that time..."

Roth's assessment was insightful. The conflict within seemed to stem from his prison-time perspective and the temptations and demands of the outside world. When Tupac was in jail, he told reporters he was a changed man. But after his release, he reverted to his old ways, talking tough and throwing gang hand signs. In many ways he appeared harder than ever before.

While in prison, Tupac said he wanted to team up with his friend Mike Tyson after he got out and start a youth organization called Us First to keep kids out of trouble. The new Tupac preached anti-violence, but he often didn't practice what he preached.

The sequence of events on the night he was shot was a reflection of the almost schizophrenic contradictions in his life. On his way to perform at a Las Vegas charity event to keep kids out of trouble and off drugs, Tupac was seen beating Orlando Anderson and kicking him while he was down. Tupac played the role of the thug up until the end. Violence had become a way of life—and death—for him.

Former *Vibe* magazine senior writer Kevin Powell began interviewing Tupac during the early stages of his career and got to know him well. Powell described his relationship with Tupac as "very intense."

"I was his biographer for a while," he said. "'Pac used to say to me all the time he wanted me to be his Alex Haley. [Haley] did the biography of Malcolm X.

"Sometimes I feel like a big brother to him, [like] I'm related to him. I miss him in a weird kind of way. You don't want to see anyone die. I think it was internal and external questions on Tupac that ultimately led to his demise. Internally he could never seem to turn that corner."

The first time Powell interviewed Tupac was in 1993.

"Even then, he felt misunderstood," Powell said. "I had been following his career since 1990 when he was with Digital Underground. It was a social commentary. I liked what he was saying. He stood out in my mind. I started collecting notes way before I got the go-ahead [to write a story] from *Vibe*. I thought, 'This is a kid who's very much the nineties. He's one person who represents the hip hop more than anybody else.'

"He was very much the period, the way James Dean was in the 1950s. He talked about dying. Always. The first piece I did with him in *Vibe*, he mentioned himself dying, and didn't want people to think he was a 'hate whitey' [person]. This kid off the bat was talking about things like that."

Powell said he doesn't know what would have become of Tupac had he lived.

"We'll never know. Tupac never really had the space to grow up, find out who he was. He was always in the public eye. The son of a famous Black Panther. He was selling drugs and trying to survive when he was young. The poverty dictated what he did. Once he had money, he was a workaholic. He never had time to take a step back. Everybody put pressure on 'Pac. Family, friends. He would have really had to take some time. He needed to step back and look at the source of that anger. He never, never got to do that. I was watching this documentary of Jimi Hendrix and it reminded me of Tupac. Everybody said [Hendrix] was dying out of frustration.

"I know from talking to people Tupac didn't even want

to go to the Tyson fight that night. He wanted to chill in California. But he was a loyalist. He told them he would go, so he went. One thing Tupac said to me—I remember saying to him, 'Why don't you just be careful,' and he said, 'There's no place like careful. If it's time to go, it's time to go.' I think that's sad. In black America some people are just waiting for death. A lot of us are like that. I'm amazed at how much people just don't care.

"The first week in December 1995 was the last time I talked to him. I really believed, based on my conversations with him in prison, that he was going to change. He talked differently about women and racial issues. But then when I interviewed him on the set of a video, weed smoke came out of the trailer and he was flashing money. I took it personally. Sometimes as a journalist you get caught up. I thought, 'God, this guy, he's not going to change.' It depressed me. I knew it was the last time I would interview him. I didn't know he would die; I just knew it was the last time.

"I think, if there's anything we can learn from Tupac it's like, man, you cannot live your life that fast and that hard and that recklessly without thinking through every decision you make. I remember thinking the last time I interviewed him, I was wishing he had still been in jail. He would have been safe from the people who not only wanted to kill him physically, but who also wanted to kill him spiritually."

Sway, the San Francisco deejay, asked Tupac where he thought he might be in five years.

"I'll have my own production company, which I'm close to right now. I'm doing my own movies," he told Sway. "I have my own restaurant, which I got right now with Suge and Snoop. I just wanna expand. I'm starting to put out some calendars for charity. I'm gonna start a little youth league in California so we can start playing some East Coast teams, some Southern teams. I wanna have like a Pop Warner League, except the rappers fund it and they're the head coaches. Have a league where you can get a big trophy with diamonds in it for a niggah to stay drug free and stay in school.

That's the only way you can be on the team. We'll have fun and eat pizza and have the finest girls there and throw concerts at the end of the year. That's what I mean by giving back."

"I see myself having a job with Death Row," Tupac continued, "being the A&R person and an artist that drop an album like Paul McCartney every five years. Not that I'm like Paul McCartney, but there's no rapper who ever did it, so that's why I use him as an example. But I wanna do it at leisure. My music will mean something and I'll drop deeper shit."

Four months after he was gunned down, Tupac Shakur was named favorite rap hip-hop artist at the American Music Awards.

6

ABOUT SUGE KNIGHT

Homicide detectives didn't learn much more than they already knew about the shooting of Tupac Shakur when they interviewed Suge Knight a few days afterwards, but they did find out what was going through his mind as he made the U-turn and drove off on Flamingo Road instead of staying at the scene of the crime when Tupac was shot. Suge told the police that his intent was to find a hospital. Had Suge not turned around, had he kept driving east on Flamingo, he would have run into Desert Springs Hospital, almost next door to Club 662 where he was headed.

One has to wonder about that, at least a little. The police did. Suge, born Marion Hugh Knight in 1965, is not unfamiliar with Las Vegas. He spent two years at the University of Nevada-Las Vegas, also located a little east of where the shooting took place. He played for the UNLV Rebels football team.

Halfway through his college career, Suge caught the attention of UNLV recruiter Wayne Nunnely, head coach of the Rebels in 1986, who later moved on to work for the National Football League's New Orleans Saints.

"You didn't really see that street roughness about him," he remembered about Suge after the shooting. (Knight had grown up on the rough streets of Compton, California.)

Suge, according to Steve Stallworth, director of sports marketing at UNLV and the starting quarterback when Suge played on the defensive line, "was all about the team." Stallworth said that his work ethic was second to none. "He never missed a practice. He was never even late for a practice."

Suge played for the Rebels in 1985 and 1986, lettering both years as a first-team defensive lineman. He earned Rookie of the Year honors and was voted All-Conference. He was also one of three player-elected captains of the team, along with teammate Eddie Wide Jr., during his senior year.

The last time Wide saw Suge was a couple of nights before Tupac was shot. They ran into each other during an evening out.

"I saw him in passing," Wide said. "He was busy, taking care of business. I saw him and we talked, basically, 'How you doing, what's up.' You know, real quick."

Before that, the last time he'd seen him had been in Irvine, California, when the two were trying out for some Canadian football teams at a combine camp—a pro-football combination camp where "different athletes are put together to showcase their talents," Wide said.

"Suge was down there and a couple of other guys [from UNLV] were there, and we sat around and talked a little bit. We talked about what to do [on the field] mostly."

Wide described Suge as "a real cool guy everyone got along well with. If he had gang ties at the time, it didn't show."

"I wouldn't know about the neighborhood he came from or the kind of guy he was before [UNLV]," he continued. "We only met each other playing ball. What happened before that time, nobody knew. I didn't know if he was a gang member or not and I didn't care. I'm not from L.A. I was raised in Vegas pretty much all my life.

"Marion was one of those guys who could—if someone had a problem, he'd talk to them. He was the kind of guy you liked to be around because he was cool. He wasn't an asshole. He wasn't cocky. He got what he gave. Marion and I got along.

We were buddies. We were the type of guys, we might go to a club together or grab something to eat. It was mostly black guys he hung out with, but he got along with everybody.

"He's got some serious talent, as far as playing ball. Very talented. We all had the same goal, and that was to play pro ball. He did what had to be done on the field. It's a lot of work and the guys on scholarships worked hard. Marion came on a full ride [scholarship]. For somebody who was that talented, he could still be in pro ball.

"The music thing, that kind of came out of the blue, because there was this one guy [on the team] named Eric Collins. Eric actually signed with Death Row later. Marion and Eric, these guys were both from L.A. Suge would always say how good Eric could rap. Eric *was* good. When Marion made the transition into music, I don't know. I was surprised at how big and how fast [Death Row] went up. With the guy's personality, you knew he was going to be successful at *something*. There were a lot of other guys getting in trouble in school. Some of the guys on our team are still in prison. To see Suge then and to see him now, I never would have predicted it, that he would be this kind of guy, the fact that he would have been in all the problems with the police, an outlaw. All the criminal activity, I never would have predicted."

Even while in college, with his sights set on becoming a professional athlete, Suge was moving toward becoming a businessman. While in school, Suge's favorite classes at UNLV were business-related, and his favorite instructor was a business teacher. His records at UNLV have been sealed, the registrar's office said, after trying to pull up his transcripts in the college's computer system.

"I can't give out any information on that student," a school clerk said. "He has a hold on it himself so nothing about him can be given out. I can't give you any information without a signed release from him."

Suge's coaches say he left UNLV his senior year, without graduating, after the football season ended. He was drafted by the Los Angeles Rams, where he played part of a season. He crossed the National Football League's picket line during a contract strike and played several games for the Rams before he was released.

He told *Vibe* magazine that he loved the game and still played sometimes, but that it wasn't meant to be for him. He had moved on.

Part of what Suge moved on to was trouble. In October 1987, Sharitha Lee Golden, mother of Suge's first child, obtained a restraining order in Los Angeles against Suge that covered her, her sister, her mother, and her aunt.

"Once I refused to talk to him, he began to threaten me and my family... tamper with my car," Golden wrote in a court document.

(Suge and Sharitha later reconciled, and according to Clark County marriage-license records, were married at the Candlelight Wedding Chapel, advertised as "the No. 1 choice of recording, stage, and movie personalities in the heart of the Las Vegas Strip," on November 3, 1989. Sharitha later headed Suge's management company, and they had a second child together.)

In November 1987, a month after Sharitha got the restraining order against Suge, he was arrested at his Las Vegas apartment for attempted murder, grand larceny auto, carrying a concealed weapon, and use of a deadly weapon to commit a crime. According to the crime report, Suge got into a fight with a man on Halloween night at Suge's home, at the Rancho Sahara Apartments at 1655 East Sahara Avenue, unit 3119.

The arrest report said that at 8 p.m. on October 31, "an altercation broke out between the above subject and another man, during which time Knight shot the victim twice—once in the wrist and once in the leg—with a handgun, and then continued to chase him. After Knight shot the victim, he then got into the victim's vehicle, which was at the scene, a 1986 Nissan Maxima... and drove away without the victim's permission to take the vehicle."

Afterward, two officers, Kathleen Alba and S. Stubbs,

were called to the apartment complex to talk to Suge, but he wasn't there. At 10 p.m., a security guard called police to tell them Suge had returned to his apartment.

Officers Alba and Stubbs returned.

"When we arrived, we saw Knight coming out of the area of his apartment and when he saw us, he turned around and walked quickly back toward his apartment door where he removed a .38 caliber revolver from inside the waistband of his pants, which was covered up by the jacket he was wearing." The Metro Police officers confiscated the .38-caliber Smith & Wesson Special.

Suge was arrested and kept overnight in a holding cell. He was booked on November 2 into the Clark County Detention Center in downtown Las Vegas at Bridger Avenue and Second Street.

Suge pleaded out to a misdemeanor in exchange for a suspended two-year sentence and was placed on three years' probation. He was fined $1,000.

Then, on June 6, 1990, Suge was charged with breaking a man's jaw in a scuffle outside a friend's house in Westside, a predominantly black area of town, when the man apparently said the wrong thing. Suge was accused of holding a gun to the man's face, while demanding an apology. The man apologized, but Suge hit him in the jaw anyway, first with his fist and then the pistol. Suge was charged with felony assault with a deadly weapon and eventually pleaded guilty, according to the court record. He received a $9,000 fine, a two-year suspended sentence, and three years' probation. The judge also ordered Suge to complete "a temper-control counseling program."

Suge Knight was neither a rapper nor a musician and had no early connection to the music industry. He was a bodyguard in Los Angeles. While working security for rhythm-and-blues singer Bobby Brown, singer-actor Whitney

Houston's husband, Suge spent a lot of time behind the scenes. He learned the ropes backstage at concerts, and was sharp enough to see an opportunity. After a while, he'd spent enough time around the L.A. rap scene to recognize its potential for making big money.

Suge became friendly with Tracy Curry, who rapped under the stage name D.O.C. and put out albums for Ruthless Records. When D.O.C. was injured in a car accident, Suge took care of him.

"I've seen Suge do some shit to some motherfuckers that's out of this world," D.O.C. told *L.A. Weekly*. "Once, we were leaving a club and I was standing there waiting for my car to come, and some nigga run up on me like he's fixin' to hit me in the jaw, and Suge just tore his ass up—broke him down to his very components. Suge was a different nigga when he was doing his business."

Suge began promoting shows in Los Angeles in 1990 and became friendly with rap producer Andre "Dr. Dre" Young, whom journalist Joe Domanick in *L.A. Weekly* called "the greatest producer and best ear in the history of hip-hop music." Dre was also under contract to Ruthless Records, but was unhappy with the label. Suge talked him into forming an alliance with him.

Ruthless Records had been formed by Eazy-E, a streetwise rapper known for his record "The Boyz N the Hood" who has since died of AIDS. Suge planned to produce an album for D.O.C., and took Dre and D.O.C. to meet Dick Griffey, the chairman and founder of Solar Records and co-founder of the television show "Soul Train." Griffey was considered a player and an insider in the record industry. Griffey and Suge reportedly intimidated Eazy-E, allegedly threatening him with pipes and baseball bats, into releasing Dre, D.O.C. and R&B singer Michel'le.

Suge denied the allegation, but the artists were released from their contracts and Suge obtained copies of the signed contract releases. Subsequently, however, Ruthless Records sent out letters to major record companies telling them that the releases were signed under duress and should not be honored. As a result, no one would sign Dre, D.O.C., or Michel'le. Suge did what he had to do: he started his own label.

"We called it Death Row 'cause most everybody had been involved with the law. A majority of our people was parolees or incarcerated. It's no joke," Suge said later.

Money, as always, was an issue. A start-up record label can cost millions to get off the ground. The company has to pay all the costs of recruiting talent, recording albums, and setting up a company infrastructure before any revenue comes in. Suge needed start-up capital.

The start-up capital was secured, if from some sources that were seemingly less than legitimate. It's been reported that Death Row has come under investigation by the Justice Department. Federal investigators are looking into, among other things, whether Death Row was launched with drug or organized-crime money. The feds are looking into whether the seed money for the record company came from Michael "Harry-O" Harris, a major investor and drug dealer, who is currently serving time on convictions for attempted murder and drug offenses. Harris' lawyer is David Kenner, who is also Death Row's attorney.

Suge has stated that corporations, such as Death Row's distributor, Westwood-based Interscope Records, were the source of the capital. Interscope for a time was owned by Time Warner. Time Warner sold its 50-percent stake in Death Row back to Interscope. Interscope, in turn, sold that share in 1996 to MCA Music Entertainment Group (now known as Universal) for a profit of roughly a hundred million dollars. Funding for day-to-day operations for the label since the beginning has been by Interscope.

Wherever the funds came from, Suge Knight and Dr. Dre signed heavyweights Snoop Doggy Dogg (Calvin Broadus), Hammer, Tha Dogg Pound, Nate Dogg, Samm Sneed, Hug, JURUPT, K-Solo, Tupac Shakur, and others, and watched them become virtual money machines. Early on, Suge had dreams of making Death Row the Motown of the nineties, and by 1995, the record company had become the largest rap label in the world. In the past few years, Death Row has grossed more than $100 million annually.

It's been said that signing with Death Row is like taking a blood oath. Death Row has been likened to a gang with Suge Knight as the kingpin or don.

"Death Row is a way of life," Suge told the *New York Times*. "It's an all-the-time thing. And ain't nobody gonna change that."

"Knight has successfully created a myth around himself as an executive not unlike a Hollywood mob figure who has strong-armed his way into the entertainment industry," Kevin Powell wrote in the October 31, 1996, issue of *Rolling Stone* magazine. "Many people inside the music business, afraid of his perceived power, were reluctant to speak on the record for this article.

Suge built his reputation on intimidation tactics. To get into Death Row's studios, most visitors would be searched for weapons; a guard at the door ran a hand-held metal detector over visitors before he'd let them in. If people in the music industry had appointments with Suge, he would often leave them waiting for hours, including top executives. It worked. People were afraid of Suge.

Knight, in a biographical profile released by Death Row, described himself as "12 o'clock."

"That's a street saying, '12 o'clock.' It means that I'm straight up and down. If I promise you I'm going to do something, you can believe it's going to happen. Mark my words, Death Row is going to be the record company of the decade."

While Dr. Dre has left to start a record label of his own, and distributor Interscope Records has severed all ties with the label, as did Time Warner, Death Row has still shown staying power. It expanded into rhythm and blues, reggae, and jazz.

Suge defended his honor in *Vibe* magazine, "My mission is helping young black talent see their dreams happen. That's my ultimate purpose in this business, so fuck anybody who can't understand or deal with that. I know how I am and what my heart is like. I leave my judgment to God."

The music industry was good to Suge. As he made more money, he spent it lavishly. He purchased thirty-four vintage and luxury cars, symbols of his wealth. He also invested in property.

On April 29, 1996, Suge purchased a four-bedroom, six-bath, 5,215-square-foot Las Vegas estate on 1.33 acres with a swimming pool for $1,625,000. The red-brick mansion, built in 1992 in the Sierra Vista Rancho Estates, sits behind Sunset Park and beside a luxury golf course in an exclusive gated community just outside the Las Vegas city limits.

Located in an area known as the Paradise Valley Township, Suge's mansion is two doors away from Mike Tyson's mansion in the horn of a cul-de-sac. Across the street is the back of singer Wayne Newton's 57-acre Shenandoah Ranch, which covers the corner and more than a city block at Tomiyasu Lane, Sunset Road, and Pecos Avenue. Friends have said Suge bought the property so he could be neighbors with Tyson. Tyson is said to have helped talk Suge into buying the house.

Suge's house was filmed in the motion picture *Casino*. It was used to shoot the home-scene footage of Frank "Lefty" Rosenthal, a mob associate and former executive of the Stardust Hotel and Casino, played by actor Robert DeNiro.

Suge lived in Las Vegas part-time and his friends and associates were frequent visitors, especially during boxing weekends. His rappers were often spotted at Club 662.

A real estate agent, who asked that her name not be used, said that after Suge purchased the residence, he "redecorated like crazy." One of the first changes he made was to paint the sides of the pool red—which promptly turned orange from exposure to the chlorine and desert sun. The deck was also red, as was the master-bedroom carpet. Suge also drove around town in a blood-red Rolls Royce Corniche.

Red is the color of the Bloods street gang.

The realtor added, "The guy wears a seven-carat diamond in his ear, and I thought, 'Oh, my God, is he for real?' He and his entourage come in [to Las Vegas] once a month and throw huge parties."

It has been widely—and incorrectly—reported that Suge owned Club 662. In fact, the nightclub, which had a county business and liquor license pending at the time of the shooting, was owned by Las Vegas businesswoman Helen Thomas, president of Platinum Road Inc. The nightclub's attorney, George Kelesis, said Suge had shown an interest in buying it. The September 7th party was allowed to be held there because of a special one-time-only permit the club was granted by the county.

Six months after Tupac's shooting, a "For Lease" sign was posted on the property, advertising it as a "restaurant/ nightclub over 10,000 square feet." The once well-manicured grounds had weeds growing through the desert landscape that surrounds the club. Dozens of cocktail glasses, some broken, were strewn on the floor in the back storage area. Just months earlier it was an exclusive by-invitation-only hotspot.

Thanks to his success, Suge Knight's world encompassed his Tarzana studio (also done up in blood red), mansions in Encino and Las Vegas, a rented penthouse in Westwood, and a house in Compton. He often drove the 300 miles from Los Angeles across the Mojave Desert via Interstate 15 to spend weekends in Las Vegas, going to prize fights and nightclubs.

But Suge's love affair with Las Vegas, which began when he was barely out of his teens, might have soured on September 7, 1996.

For Suge Knight, on his way to a benefit party at Club 662 with his friend and main hit-maker, Tupac Shakur, by his side, Las Vegas must have represented everything good about the world. A few violent moments later, as Tupac's blood spilled from three bullet holes, it surely must have seemed like hell itself. Las Vegas is good for some and bad for others, with nothing in between.

Knight said he waited four days after the shooting of Tupac Shakur to talk to detectives because he needed time to collect his thoughts and to recover from the minor head wound he received. Two days after his meeting with homicide detectives, on the day Tupac died, David Chesnoff, one of his Las Vegas attorneys, drove Suge downtown to Sixth Street. Chesnoff said it was the FBI who "reminded" Suge he needed to register as an ex-con. The 300-pound ex-linebacker walked into the fingerprint section of the Metropolitan Police and registered for the first time with the state of Nevada as a convicted felon.

A long-time Nevada state law requires felons to register within 72 hours of arriving in the state. "Probably because of gaming," surmised Elizabeth Wright, supervisor of Metro's convicted-person registration office. "They want to keep track of people coming into the state, the ones who have convictions."

Metro police admittedly give preferential treatment to celebrities, at least when they register as felons. They're given the red-carpet treatment by the director of the section. Famous people don't have to stand in line for thirty minutes to three hours like the general public. If they make a phone call in advance telling the director's office they'll be coming in, they're ushered through a back entrance so they don't have to mingle with the common folk. That's what Mike Tyson did after he was released from prison after serving out his sentence for a sexual assault conviction.

Suge was fingerprinted, his mug shot was taken, and he was interviewed by investigators. Police then ran his name in two national databases to see whether he had any new arrests or convictions. He was issued a wallet-sized convicted-felon card to carry with him.

• • •

Death Row issued a statement after Tupac's murder. "Suge Knight and the entire Death Row Records family are saddened by the passing of our brother and star rap recording artist Tupac Amaru Shakur," the company said officially.

"If I could change things, I would give up Death Row, I would give up this lifestyle, I would give up a life to bring him back," Knight told the *Los Angeles Times*. "Me and Tupac was joined at the hip."

Knight told reporter Jordan Pelaez that Tupac spoke to him from his death bed. "We were in the hospital, and I was sittin' on the bed, and he called out to me and said he loved me," Suge told Pelaez.

To another reporter he said, "I miss him. I had a lot of love for him, and I miss him."

And to "America's Most Wanted" television show, Suge said, "I loved 'Pac then, I love 'Pac now. He loved me. That's my little homey, and it's always going to be that way, you know? And nothing's going to change that.

"September 7 is a part of history. It's a sad day. It's an educational day."

However, also on "America's Most Wanted," in an interview two months after Tupac died, Detective Mike Franks described Suge's shortcomings as an eyewitness. "He's a hands-on witness. He's two feet farther away than Tupac, and he sees nothing," Franks said. "We spent three days just trying to get him [to talk to us]. I mean, this is a guy joined at the hip with Tupac? He's not that joined at the hip. He didn't try too hard."

Detective Brent Becker agreed, saying, "I know that some of these witnesses idolized this man. But they obviously didn't care for him enough to help bring in his murderers, and that's a pretty sad state of affairs."

• • •

Suge Knight's state of affairs definitely took a turn for the worse the fateful evening of Saturday, September 7, 1996. Rumors were already swirling about trouble at Death Row, and now he'd lost his top moneymaker, Tupac Shakur. Some have gone so far as to say Death Row was on the brink of failure.

Afeni Shakur has since filed a $17 million lawsuit against Death Row relating to her son's estate. Afeni has been negotiating with Death Row and a large settlement is said to be imminent.

The FBI and two grand juries were reportedly investigating Death Row Records and Suge Knight, looking for links to drug trafficking and money laundering with Los Angeles street gangs and the New York Mafia. The feds, reportedly, were investigating Suge's association with Michael "Harry O" Harris and Ricardo Crockett.

A Los Angeles deputy district attorney was investigated by the California state attorney general's office for "unusual ties" to Death Row and Suge.

And Death Row had reportedly fallen behind in meeting deadlines to deliver five albums that were scheduled to be released in the fourth quarter of 1996, the most profitable time of the year for record companies.

Worst of all, Suge himself had lost his freedom.

In 1995 Suge Knight pleaded no contest to assaulting two rap entertainers at a Hollywood studio, was placed on five years probation, and warned to stay off drugs and to obey all laws. By taking part in the beating of Orlando Anderson at the MGM Grand the night Tupac was shot, a Superior Court judge ruled that Knight had violated his probation order.

In court just before he was sentenced, Suge made a statement to Superior Court Judge J. Stephen Czuleger:

"I been through a lot this year. I lost my best friend. A lot of people don't realize how it is to lose a best friend. I always wanted a little brother, and now he's not here.

"As far as the situation with the fight, I'm not trying to open up the case or go back to the incident in Vegas, but I wanna stipulate on that because it's important to me, 'cause I gotta live with this. When Anderson came up to testify—I'd be the first to say he's not a friend of mine. And to be honest, I felt that this guy could play with the truth and go against me just to lie. But since he was under oath, I felt he told the truth.

"Your honor, I was breakin' up the fight. I knew I was on probation. I put my freedom and my life on the line. And I feel if I wouldn't have stopped that fight—I'm not saying the same person who came and shot us later was these type of people, but if they was, instead of me getting shot in my head and one person dead, it could have been 30 people dead in Vegas at the MGM.

"And even at the end, Your Honor, when everybody say, 'It was a kick,' it wasn't a kick. I admit that I was breaking up a fight, and I admit I was frustrated, but at the same time, it's not a nine-year kick. This guy wasn't harmed, wasn't anything broke on him. If you ask anybody that seen me fight, Your Honor, the first they'd tell you is, 'That guy wouldn't be standing there giving statements.' When I fights, sir, I fights.

"But I've changed my life to get away from fighting. And I wanna enlighten not just you, but the courtroom, because my family is here. And it might be the last time I speak to my family. I could go to jail and anything could happen. But I'm not here for the judge to feel pity for me. I'm just speaking from my heart.

"I'm not gonna waste any more of the court's time, but I just thought it was important that I get this off my chest and address the court the way I feel."

Despite his plea for mercy and his team of attorneys' earlier filing of motion after motion, on February 28, 1997, Czuleger handed down a long prison term.

"The defendant is sentenced to nine years in state prison,"

he told the court. Then he turned to Knight and said, "You did blow it."

No one else involved in the Orlando Anderson beating on September 7, 1996, was arrested or charged in connection with the incident. The greatest irony is, officially, the incident never happened. Metro Police did not file a crime report, therefore there was no crime. Suge was sentenced to nine years of hard time for something for which no official record exists.

Suge's life today is a far cry from the high-flying days when the Hip Hop Nation's largest rap label produced records from the world's top rap artist. On March 12, 1997, four months after his arrest, Suge was taken by a prison bus from Los Angeles county's central jail to Delano, California, where he was incarcerated at the North Kern State Prison near Bakersfield, housed as prisoner No. K43480. Suge was placed in the reception wing—DC6 unit, cell No. 229L—awaiting permanent housing.

On May 21, 1997, Suge was transferred to the California Men's Colony East. The prison, off State Highway 101 three miles west of San Luis Obispo and nine miles east of Morro Bay, is a medium- to high-security facility. Two prisons there (East and West) house 6,500 inmates. Suge was placed in the East prison because of his notoriety and for his safety, according to prison spokeswoman Terri Knight (no relation). The facility has armed security and a double-fence line surrounding it. Other celebrities incarcerated there in the past have included Christian Brando, Ike Turner, Thomas "Hollywood" Henderson (a former linebacker for the Dallas Cowboys convicted of drug-related crimes), and several members of the Charles Manson family.

To get privileges within the prison system (such as phone use, quarterly packages from family members, and canteen privileges for snack foods), inmates must work in a prison-industry factory, making state license plates, prison-issue T-shirts and shoes, textile products and socks, work boots for forestry crews, and jackets. Inmates also have the option of going to school, but the privileges are better from the factory work.

Suge is allowed to have non-contact visits four days a week with people who are approved by the prison, including his team of attorneys. He'll be eligible for parole after two to three years (depending on "good-time" credits he may earn).

Meanwhile, now that he's incarcerated in a state prison, California law prohibits Suge Knight from running Death Row Records. Knight's wife Sharitha, from whom he amicably separated, has been taking care of the day-to-day operation of Death Row since Suge's incarceration.

7

YAFEU FULA'S MURDER

Yafeu Fula was gunned down in the hallway of a federal housing project in Irvington, New Jersey, two months after Tupac Shakur was murdered.

Yaasmyn Fula, one of Afeni Shakur's best friends, lost her only son in that shooting. Metro Police lost their only willing witness to Tupac's murder.

Fula toured with Outlaw Immortalz, formerly called Thug Life, a quartet that regularly backed Tupac in concert and appeared with him on the first album he cut for Death Row, *All Eyez On Me*. All the back-up players had the words "THUG LIFE" tattooed, like Tupac, across their mid-abdomen sections. Tupac planned to produce records for the group under his newly formed company, Euphanasia. Tupac hired Fula's mother Yaasmyn to manage the L.A.-based company.

Fula, just 19 years old, was a passenger in the Lexus that was directly behind Suge's BMW when the shooting occurred. Bodyguard and former peace officer Frank Alexander was driving the Lexus; neither he nor rapper Malcolm Greenridge, the other passenger, admitted to seeing the assailant. Only Fula told police he might be able to pick out Tupac's shooter from a photo lineup. He was the only witness that night who exhibited a willingness to help the police.

"Yafeu Fula was the only one who gave us an indication in the interview he could identify the gunman," Lieutenant Wayne Petersen said. "His statement was, 'Yeah, I might be able to recognize him.'"

But in the aftermath of the shooting, detectives were frustrated by not being able to schedule an interview with Fula. Once Fula left Las Vegas, detectives were referred to Death Row attorney David Kenner, the same lawyer they dealt with when they tried to schedule an interview with Suge Knight.

Before a meeting could be arranged, Fula, too, was murdered.

On Sunday, November 13, 1996, at 3:48 a.m., Fula was fatally shot in the face at point-blank range while in a hallway of a housing project in Irvington, New Jersey, where his girlfriend lived. Found slumped against a wall, he was taken by ambulance to University Hospital in Newark, New Jersey. Efforts to save his life were futile, and he was pronounced dead at 1 p.m.

There were reports that Fula had been wearing a flak jacket when he was found. Bruce "Fatal" Washington, a fellow rapper in Outlaw Immortalz, told reporters that Fula and the other members of the rap group frequently wore bulletproof vests for protection, especially in the wake of Tupac's murder.

Like Tupac, Fula was shot following a Mike Tyson heavyweight prize fight, slain just hours after the Mike Tyson-Evander Holyfield fight in Las Vegas.

Within two days of the murder, Orange police arrested and charged two teenagers. Police said the case was not related to Tupac's murder. Publicly, Las Vegas police, too, have insisted that there was no relation. Sergeant Manning attributes Fula's death in part to the general nature of being a young black male in this country today.

Statistics show that black-on-black gun violence has been the leading cause of death for black youths 15 to 19 years old since 1969. From 1987 to 1989, the gun homicide rate for African-American males 15 to 19 years old increased 71 percent.

Of the roughly 20,000 murders committed each year in the United States between 1991 and 1995, 50 percent were cases involving black victims.

Privately, Las Vegas police say that while their sense is that the case probably is related, they have to go on the evidence, not a gut feeling. The criminal justice system demands that when police submit a case to the district attorney's office, the evidence must be strong enough for it to be approved for criminal prosecution. Manning says he can't go on instinct and he can't go on a gut feeling. Still, it's hard to imagine that a possible star witness to a murder who gets gunned down just two months later isn't connected to the original case.

Having been intimately involved with this story for months, I recognized the connection the minute I heard about it, and broke the story.

I was working on Monday, November 14, making my rounds on the phone as I do every day. Since I work for an afternoon daily, I'm on deadline each morning for that day's edition. I made a routine phone call to homicide to see if there was anything new in the Shakur investigation and was told that detectives had sketchy information that a witness in the case had been murdered back East; homicide had gotten a message overnight on its answering machine. The investigator didn't know how to spell Yafeu Fula's name. He didn't know the name of the city where the witness was murdered. He did know that it happened somewhere in New Jersey.

I hung up and immediately relayed what little I knew to the city desk and was told to see what I could get. Meantime, the copy desk freed up space on the front page just in case the story panned out.

I picked cities at random, phoned directory assistance for the numbers, and then, one by one, called about 10 police departments; the last one had heard there'd been a murder in Orange, New Jersey. I called the police department there and asked for the homicide division. An officer confirmed that there had been a murder the day before. The captain who could tell me about it, however, was in a meeting, unavailable to speak with me. No one else there was authorized to talk to the press. The officer invited me to attend an afternoon news conference. I told him that I was in Las Vegas and needed information for that day's paper. He said he'd heard the homicide was mentioned in one of the area's newspapers, but he didn't know which one. So I called the papers. I reached a reporter at the *Star-Ledger* in Orange, New Jersey.

The newspaper reported that Yafeu Fula, a back-up singer for Tupac, had been shot to death. Wire services had not moved the story overnight.

The connection had not been made—nor reported—that Fula was a key witness in Tupac's murder and now he too was dead. Orange Police Captain Richard Conte called me a few minutes later with the details. The captain told me he wasn't aware that Fula was a witness to a murder.

My paper, the *Las Vegas Sun*, bannered the story on the front page. The article began, "A key witness Metro Police have been trying to interview since the fatal shooting of rapper Tupac Shakur has been murdered in New Jersey." The Associated Press picked up the piece and it was the lead story on local and national TV news programs that evening.

Officially, Las Vegas' Metro Police and police in Orange, New Jersey claimed that Fula's murder was not connected to Tupac's murder. "It doesn't appear at this time to be involved with the Tupac Shakur killing," Captain Conte told reporters who followed up on the story.

When I pressed him about the Las Vegas connection, Conte said Fula knew the two people who shot him and that it may have been drug-related.

"I think it's more or less a lifestyle-related homicide, as opposed to Death Row versus Biggie and all that," Conte said. "The availability that people have of drugs and guns—I think he died because of that, not because he saw Tupac Shakur killed. It was a lifestyle thing. [Fula] was going out with a girl there. He was at her apartment."

Conte noted, "In talking to California and Las Vegas detectives, I do not believe it was related to either Tupac Shakur or gang affiliation. With the evidence at hand, I can say it's not gang-related."

Kevin Manning, as well, maintained there was no evidence to link Fula's killing with his being a witness in Tupac's murder. "Based on the information we received from Orange Police, we don't think there's a connection," Manning said. Metro homicide detectives never went to New Jersey to interview the murder suspects.

Within 48 hours, the two teenagers—16- and 17-year-old black youths—were charged with Fula's murder. Their names were not released because of their ages. Both have pleaded not guilty. They have yet to go to trial.

Even though Yafeu Fula was Metro's best witness in Tupac's murder case, Metro Lieutenant Larry Spinosa said, "He wasn't coming forward anyway. We didn't know where he was until he turned up dead in New Jersey. We wanted Fula to look at a photo lineup, and the attorney would say he would get back to us, and he never did. As far as the investigation is concerned, it really does not change the status in the case at all. It's an open investigation. However, at this point, we've reached an end to fresh leads."

8

BIGGIE SMALLS' MURDER

On Sunday, March 9, 1997, East Coast rap superstar Biggie Smalls, also known as Notorious B.I.G., was attending a star-studded party in Los Angeles to celebrate the 11th Annual Soul Train Music Awards. He'd been in Los Angeles for about two weeks doing West Coast interviews and had canceled a flight to Europe so he could attend the post-awards get-together. The party, held at the Petersen Automotive Museum in the mid-Wilshire district of Los Angeles and sponsored by *Vibe* magazine, Qwest Records, and Tangueray, was supposed to have been private, but by the time Biggie and his associates and friends arrived, about 2,000 people had filed into the museum.

Biggie, six-foot-three and weighing upwards of 300 pounds, wore a black suede shirt and a solid gold chain around his neck with a large gold cross hanging from it. He was celebrating his award, "Lyricist of the Year." But he was unhappy that he hadn't won the "Dopest Rhyme of the Month," an award given by *The Source* magazine.

"See, I want you to be able to say, 'Big, without hesitation, he's the best,'" he told a reporter for *The Source*.

Biggie was also anticipating the release of his second CD, *Life After Death...'Til Death Do Us Part*, in two weeks. The disc jockey played a single, "Hypnotize," off the new album. Biggie talked about the new release in an interview with BET (Black Entertainment Television). "If you thought the [first] album was a fluke, hold your head, 'cause this next one, man, it's all. It's all like you never thought. The next album is called 'Life After Death' and we ain't takin' no prisoners."

Most of the evening, Biggie sat with Russell Simmons, president and CEO of Def Jam Records, and his producer, Sean Combs, CEO of Biggie's record label, Bad Boy Entertainment, who records under the name of Puff Daddy and whom his friends call Puffy. Actor Wesley Snipes and singer Seal, among others, were also there. Women danced for Biggie at his table. He was having a good time.

Shortly after midnight, a fire marshal arrived at the museum, went inside, and abruptly broke up the party, because the crowd was far in excess of the building's capacity per the city's fire code.

At 12:35 a.m., Biggie left the building and climbed into the passenger seat of his rented GMC Suburban (he didn't have a driver's license). On the bumper of Biggie's Suburban was a sticker that read "Think B.I.G. March 25, 1997," which was a promotion for his upcoming CD. His bodyguard and driver, D-Rockefeller (D-Rock), was behind the wheel; his backup singer and protege, Li'l Caesar from Junior M.A.F.I.A., was in the backseat (D-Rock, Li'l Caesar, and Biggie were roommates in a New Jersey bachelor pad). Another Suburban with Biggie's entourage was in front, carrying Puffy Combs. Behind Biggie's Suburban was a Chevy Blazer, carrying security guards.

Biggie's GMC left the parking lot and D-Rock made a right turn onto Fairfax Avenue. All three cars were stopped at a red light at the Wilshire Boulevard intersection when a dark-colored car pulled alongside the GMC's passenger side. Moments later, the driver of the dark car stuck a 9-millimeter weapon out the window and opened fire. Six to ten shots were fired from the handgun. Biggie was hit seven times in the chest and abdomen.

He lost consciousness almost immediately.

Puffy Combs said he heard the crack of gunfire that killed Biggie. "I jumped out of my car and ran over to his," Combs told the *New York Daily News*. He fell to his knees at his friend's lifeless body, begging for God to help him. "I was saying the Lord's Prayer and Hail Marys. I was begging God to help him out. I was touching him and talking to him in his ear."

Puffy and D-Rock tried to move Biggie, but he was too heavy. Instead, Puffy propped him up in the passenger seat and closed the Suburban's door. D-Rock got back into the driver's seat, Puffy got in the back seat, and they took Biggie to Cedars-Sinai Medical Center. When they arrived at the hospital, they helped emergency personnel lift Biggie's lifeless body onto a stretcher.

But Biggie Smalls was dead on arrival. Hospital officials said Biggie probably died immediately after being shot. At 1:15 a.m., he was pronounced dead at Cedars-Sinai, the same hospital were Eazy-E had died of AIDS.

Biggie was buried Tuesday, March 18, in his native New York City. With thousands cheering along the route, his casket was driven through the impoverished streets of Bedford-Stuyvesant where he was raised. Some onlookers jumped onto parked cars and began dancing to Biggie's music, blaring from ghetto blasters. Ten people were arrested for disorderly conduct.

The similarities in the lives and deaths of Tupac Shakur and Biggie Smalls are striking.

Like Tupac, Christopher Wallace was born in Brooklyn and grew up on the streets of "Bed-Stuy." They were both raised by single mothers. Biggie's mother, Voletta Wallace, a Jamaican national, was a preschool teacher. His father, also Jamaican, left when Christopher was two. But unlike Tupac's troubled and impoverished childhood, Voletta Wallace has said her son had a stable upbringing.

Mrs. Wallace told *Spin* magazine that her son was once on the honor roll at a Catholic school. "According to what I've read, he's some hooligan from a single-parent household in a run-down ghetto walk-up. Well, let me tell you, there are plenty of intelligent, good-hearted kids from single-parent homes, and I always had a beautiful apartment. He has never gone hungry."

Tupac, too, had been a good student.

Despite his mother's best efforts, Biggie succumbed to the lures of the street. He dropped out of high school to sell drugs. So did Tupac.

"When he quit school, I wanted to kill him," Voletta said. "Finally, when he was 18, I said, 'If you can't live by my rules, you can't live under my roof.' I don't care if I was cold. If I had to do it all over again, I would."

"I was full-time, a hundred percent hustler," says one of Biggie's rap songs. "Sellin' drugs, waking up early in the morning, hitting the set selling any shit till the crack of dawn. My mother goin' to work would see me out there in the morning. That's how I was on it."

Biggie and Tupac each lived the life of a street gangster before either got into the music business. Biggie went from the street to the studio. He made his debut on Mary J. Blige's remixes of "Real Love" and "What's the 411?" He appeared in Supercat's video, "Dolly My Baby." His first single was "Party and Bullshit." His first album, *Ready to Die*, went platinum for Bad Boy Entertainment, selling more than one million copies. He was honored as "Rap Artist of the Year" at the 1995 Billboard Awards.

"He was the king of rap on the East Coast, definitely, without a question," said rap music promoter Peter Thomas, during a "Prime Time Live" interview.

Like Tupac, Biggie had trouble with the law (though not nearly as serious). On September 15, 1996, two days after Tupac died, Biggie was busted for smoking marijuana while sitting in his parked luxury car on a Brooklyn street. He was charged with drug possession. He'd also been arrested for weapons and assault involving a show promoter in Camden.

Most bizarre, however, both Biggie and Tupac predicted their own deaths in their last albums, both of which were released posthumously. In his song "You're Nobody," he raps, "You're nobody, Till somebody kills you." Both Tupac's *Makaveli* and Biggie's *Life After Death* sold out the first week. Biggie's final album surpassed the Beatles' last album in record sales.

As in life, so too in death.

Both Tupac and Biggie were gunned down in drive-by shootings—Tupac was 25 when he was killed, Biggie was 24. Both had hired off-duty cops to guard them the night they were killed. Lieutenant Ross Moen of the Los Angeles Police Department's Wilshire division, which is handling Biggie's murder investigation, said the Blazer carrying Biggie's security guards chased after the gunman's vehicle for a few blocks but lost it before they could get a license plate number. The same thing happened after the Tupac shooting; several cars chased after the Cadillac, police said, but none were able to catch it. Or if they did, they didn't report it to the cops.

When Tupac was shot, his record-label owner, Suge Knight, drove him away from the crime scene, heading for a hospital. When Biggie was shot, his record-label CEO, Puffy Combs, told his bodyguard to drive away from the scene, heading for a hospital.

Also similar to the Tupac shooting, Biggie's murder was witnessed by scores of people. Biggie's estranged wife, Faith, dozens of partygoers, security guards, and parking attendants witnessed the shooting. But just as in the Las Vegas investigation of Tupac's murder, police initially said they had no description of the gunman and that witnesses were afraid to talk. And just like in Tupac's drive-by, no one took down the license plate of the car.

"It's frustrating," Detective Raymond Futami, one of 20 investigators assigned to the case, said in a published report. "I'm sure there's a little bit of an intimidation factor...because of the reputation of some of the people who are involved in this case."

Two witnesses were able to help police. Unlike the members of Tupac's entourage, two of the men sitting with Biggie in his Suburban that night provided enough information for a police artist to sketch a detailed composite drawing. The drawing shows a black man with a heart-shaped face, a light trimmed mustache, and a receding hairline. He was wearing an Oxford shirt and a dark bow tie. Moen described the suspect as a "young male African-American in his early twenties." The drawing was circulated nationwide. Police have also said they believe the gunman had an accomplice.

Early on, investigators considered the theory that Biggie Smalls' death may have been payback for Tupac Shakur's slaying.

"We believe it was gang-related," said Lieutenant Moen. "We believe that it was premeditated, that he was targeted for the purpose of killing him. The way it went down, it was a targeted hit."

Lieutenant Moen added during a news conference: "We're investigating possible connections to other murders in New York, Atlanta, and L.A. We can't ignore the fact that there have been a number of murders involving rap singers recently."

About two weeks after the shooting, L.A. police seized a videotape in Houston they felt could help them find Biggie's assailant.

"We expect the tape to give us some key information. We're hoping the tape is going to assist in having people come forward to identify the shooter for us," Moen told the *Houston Chronicle*. A Houston woman, who spoke to the newspaper on condition of anonymity, told the *Chronicle* the tape was filmed by a group of Houston residents who were in Los Angeles for the Soul Train Music awards. In a follow-up phone call, Moen said he couldn't reveal what detectives learned from viewing the videotape, because it was evidence in the ongoing investigation.

L.A. Homicide Detective Harper (who wouldn't give his

first name), said, "The tape is just one in a million things we're doing in the investigation."

There were rumors that Biggie was under federal surveillance just before the shooting, but they were unsubstantiated and probably not true, according to L.A.P.D.'s Lieutenant Pat Conman.

"I have no idea what the feds are doing, but to my knowledge, that's not true," Conman said in a telephone interview. "I have no knowledge that Biggie Smalls was under surveillance by the feds."

But the *Los Angeles Times* reported that undercover officers from New York were in the vicinity at the time of the shooting as part of a federal investigation of criminals thought to have connections to Bad Boy Entertainment.

Conman also said that members of Las Vegas Metro Police's homicide team investigating Tupac's murder had been in touch with L.A.P.D. detectives about Biggie's murder, "but just in the normal course of business. I believe detectives have had some conversations with them. They're following the case."

Unlike investigators in Tupac's murder case, Los Angeles police have been optimistic about cracking Biggie's homicide and have publicly said that they expect to make an arrest.

"I can tell you we are going to make an arrest," Lieutenant Moen said at a news conference two weeks after Biggie's slaying. "I cannot tell you when we are going to make that arrest. There's a lot left to be done yet in this investigation."

But six weeks after Biggie's death, homicide Lieutenant Conman admitted that nothing new had come up in the case.

"We have just a few leads we're following up," Conman told me. "There's nothing startling to report."

Detective Harper pointed out that "People are afraid and don't want to talk to us. People [rappers] have careers to look after."

In stark contrast to the Tupac investigation (and Metro's three-man homicide team), L.A.P.D. assigned a team of 20 investigators, who identified and interviewed nearly 200 witnesses.

"We didn't need any more," Metro's Manning insisted. "They [L.A. police] gathered as much information in their case, with all their people, as we did in ours. The more people involved, the more things [information] get lost. You have a communications problem."

As of this writing, the same number of investigators were still working on both cases, and Manning's statement appears accurate. Whether they were throwing three investigators or twenty at the respective cases, neither Metro nor the L.A.P.D. have closed either murder.

Biggie and Tupac once counted each other as friends. The two had a falling out after Tupac accused Biggie of copying his style and of setting him up in the 1994 robbery at Quad Studios in Manhattan, where Tupac was shot the first time. Biggie was in the building recording an album at the time.

According to San Francisco deejay Sway, "The Biggie thing, Tupac told me, is what he heard. He knew Biggie didn't pull the trigger [at the Manhattan studio shooting]. There were allegations in the air that Biggie had something to do with it, but I don't think Tupac knew who did it."

When Tupac was in jail, he got letters from people saying Biggie's homeboys had something to do with the shooting. In Tupac's mind, that scenario grew stronger as more and more people told him that. And the two were at odds with each other ever since. Their record labels were rivals during the same time. As early as 1994, Biggie told the *Chicago Tribune*, "I'm scared to death. Scared of getting my brains blown out."

By then bitter enemies, Tupac and Biggie taunted each other, and they used their music to do it.

After accusing Biggie of stealing his lyrics, Tupac went out and stole Biggie's wife, or at least he claimed to have slept with Faith Evans (Biggie and Faith were separated; Biggie had been dating rapper Li'l Kim when he died).

Tupac rapped, "I fucked your bitch, you fat motherfucker. You claim to be a player, but I fucked your wife."

Biggie rapped right back in his solo album, "Dumb rappers need teachin', Lesson A, don't fuck with B-I-G, that's that." But Biggie claimed the lyrics had nothing to do with Tupac.

In a Miramax documentary titled "Rhyme or Reason," Biggie talked about his dispute with Tupac and said it was just a coincidence.

"We two individual people, you know what I'm saying?" he said. "One man against one man made a whole West Coast hate a whole East Coast, and vice versa."

The situation with Tupac was "blown up to much more than it was," he told *The Source* magazine. "They'd gone and made a personal beef between me and [Tupac and Death Row] into a coastal beef, East against West. And that's crazy. That's bananas right there." He said he still planned to go to California because "they got the women...the weed...and the weather.

He blamed the media for the hype.

"I never did nothin' wrong to nobody," he said. "I ain't' never did nothin' wrong to Tupac, I ain't never did nothin' wrong to Faith... And I kept quiet. I kept my mouth shut. I figure if I had been the one sittin' here riffin' it'd seem like I'd had a point to prove. I know I ain't done nothin' so it don't make no sense for me to say nothin'. I just let everybody do they thing."

After Tupac was killed, Biggie told *Spin* magazine's Sia Michel, "I had nothing to do with any of that Tupac shit. That's a complete and total misconception. I definitely wouldn't wish death on anyone. I'm sorry he's gone—that dude was nice on the mike."

For his part, Tupac, in a *Vibe* magazine interview, described Biggie as his brother.

"Regardless of all this stuff—no matter what he say, what

I say—Biggie's still my brother. He's black. He's my brother. We just have a conflict of interest. We have a difference of opinion," he said.

"I don't want it to be about violence. I want it to be about money. I told Suge my idea: Bad Boy make a record with all the East Coast niggas. Death Row make a record with all the West Coast niggas. We drop the records on the same day. Whoever sell the most records, that's who the bombest. And then we stop battling. We could do pay-per-views for charity, for the community.

"That's as together as we can get. For money. What about getting together as black men? We are together as black men— they over there, we over here. If we really gonna live in peace, we all can't be in the same room."

Writer Kevin Powell said he thought Biggie was an unfortunate innocent bystander in the Death Row-Bad Boy feud.

"Suge definitely encouraged that," Powell said. "It sells records, definitely. What record label—think about it—when in the history of music has a song like 'Hit 'Em Up' been put out? People heard the record. It was ridiculous. Tupac says he slept with Biggie's wife, Faith. There's a song on Biggie's new album. It's called 'Notorious Thug.' He says, 'I have a so-called beef with you-know-who.' He doesn't even say Tupac's name.

"I really feel deep down in my heart that Biggie just happened to be an innocent bystander and he caught the brunt of it," Powell said in a telephone interview from Brooklyn. "Black kids, the young black people on the East Coast, are very different from the West. I can go to Harlem, I can go to Staten Island or Queens. It's not like a big deal. We've never claimed East Coast like they claim West Coast in California. New York is not the East Coast; you have Connecticut, Florida, other states. I know for a fact that a lot of kids in the East love West Coast music. I do. Biggie was the first East Coast artist in a long time who was able to transcend those boundaries. People here are petrified of going to California at this point. No one knows where it's coming from. The running joke is, whoever is mentioned in Tupac's last album, they are scared to death. You don't know who's doing the killings. You don't know where it's coming from. It's scary, man."

KMEL's Sway said, "The media has done a very poor job of reporting the truth and kind of printed what they wanted to print in order to sell papers. There's no such thing as an East-West war. There are individuals who had conflicts. It's not the coast of a country against a coast of a country. It's easier to print that. The coasts are divided by the media."

"It's a sad world where you can't even go to the other coast and go out and enjoy a party like everyone else because you think somebody's going to kill you," commented Peter Thomas, a rap music promoter. "You're not just talking to an individual. You're talking to a complete community, and in that community there's a lot of people who have absolutely no sense, but they do have a forty-five."

"For a rap superstar," wrote Sia Michel in *Spin* magazine, "Biggie's dreams were almost embarrassingly small: His ideal future, he said, was 'to quit the game and just chill and watch my kids grow up—live the life of a normal rich person.' That became an impossibility the day Tupac Shakur declared war on [Biggie]…"

Just before he was killed, Biggie told *The Source* magazine he'd thought about quitting the game of rap, commenting that he was laying low because, "I could fuck around and get murdered out in these streets.

"It's a headache…Sometimes as of late, I've really been talkin' about quittin'. I really want to stop. If I was financially stable I would. I figure if I was to make like a cool ten or fifteen million, I could; probably just chill and put my artists out on my label and help them out more, but just not make any more music. I would quit." He talked about relocating from the East Coast to the South "where I can just move at my pace and not really have anybody movin' at the same pace as me. Or where I can just do what I want to do and it wouldn't seem strange to other people. I just wanna be in a calm area. I just wanna be able to relax."

Sway conducted one of Biggie's last interviews on the air. Sway said, "Biggie talked about Puffy being instrumental in him finding God in his life. He talked about his child. He had a baby. He talked about music and trying to be one of the best rappers. It was real important that he get respect as an emcee. I don't think he had no idea what was going to hit him. He wouldn't have been parading around like that in L.A. if he did."

No arrests have been made and Biggie Smalls' murder remains unsolved.

9

GANGSTA RAP AND
THE RECORD COMPANIES

Rap began as a beat in the streets, and word play. It draws its roots from the Jamaican art form known as "toasting." Early rapper DJ Kool Herc said that "the whole chemistry of rap came from Jamaica. I was born in Jamaica and I was listening to American music in Jamaica. In Jamaica, all you needed was a drum and bass. My music is all about heavy bass."

In the early days, when rap was getting started, the rhyming was added. Its authentic from-the-street lyrics were crucial to rap's success. Rap developed into an East Coast cultural phenomenon, which included grafitti and break dancing.

"[For me], the rhyming came about because I liked playing lyrics that were saying something," DJ Kool Herc said. "I figured people would pick it up by me playing those records, but at the same time I would say something myself with a meaningful message to it."

Herc identifies the first rappers, besides himself, as Coke La Rock (whose first stage name was A-1 Coke), Timmy Tim, Clark Kent, and Bo King, all American rappers. Artists such as James Brown, the Last Poets, and Gil Scott Heron helped influence rap's early years.

Surfacing in the seventies, rap was a vibrant provocative new musical form from America's urban black community. It has progressed into different sounds and different avenues. It's free-style music, a form of electro funk—music with a beat in the background and an emcee, a rhymer, rapping to it in front.

The first real hip-hop song, "Rapper's Delight" by Henry "Big Banle" Hanle, broke into the mainstream in 1979 under the first hip-hop label, Sugarhill Gang. Hanle was a club bouncer who started emceeing and rapping in a New Jersey pizzeria. Early hip-hop rappers were Melle Mel, Grand Master Flash, and Rakim. Rakim was one of the first to rap about the living conditions of African-Americans and Latinos. (The trend continues today. Tupac Shakur often said his music showed how he and others like him *really* lived in the ghetto and in the streets.)

In 1987, the music industry for the first time recognized rap music by giving it a separate category at the American Music Awards. It elevated rap to the mainstream.

Hip hop became the term for the culture surrounding rap music. *True* hip-hop, say those in the music industry, evolved from beebop in the 1950s. Rapping (or emceeing), scratching records, break dancing, and graffiti art are all part of the hip-hop culture. How the rappers act, walk, look, and talk are also a large part of the culture; without that, the music is colorless, rappers say. Like rap, hip-hop was popularized in the mid-'70s, particularly in the South Bronx section of New York City. It has thrived within the African-American and Puerto Rican communities in New York. It's referred to today as the culture of the Hip Hop Nation.

In the late 1980s, "gangsta" rap splintered off from the larger hip-hop/rap culture. The lyrics borrowed heavily from the '60s and '70s themes of sex, drugs, and rock 'n' roll—with a violent new twist: a primary focus on gangs and weapons. New words and phrases infused the style, such as "gats" (19th-century Gatling guns), gang wars, bitches and ho's, "blunts" (fat marijuana joints or cigars), 40-ouncers (bottles of malt liquor), and "25 with an L" (25 years to life in prison).

Some credit Philadelphia's Schooly D as being the original hard-core gangsta rapper. Others claim the hard-core rap style was officially launched with Ice-T's *Rhyme Pays* album in 1987.

On the East Coast, Def Jam's LL Cool J, Public Enemy, and the Beastie Boys (who are white) brought gangsta rap into the mainstream. Compton's N.W.A. (Niggaz With Attitude) pioneered gangsta rap on the West Coast. Dr. Dre, who later founded Death Row Records with Suge Knight, was an early member of N.W.A.

Gangsta rap, which chronicles the bleak and often violent way of life of the residents of the nation's toughest black neighborhoods, has increasingly sparked controversy since it emerged in the late 1980s and early 1990s. Much of the controversy has centered on the violence-packed lyrics. The music industry, insisting it is defending artistic freedom and arguing that music doesn't cause violence, has weathered a storm of criticism. Some of the criticism has been prompted by a practice of the record companies of hiring rappers with criminal backgrounds.

The gangsta rap rivalry developed in the 1980s when West Coast rappers grew more popular, surpassing the record sales of East Coast rappers. Biggie Smalls, who built his gangsta rap persona around a troubled past that included his admitted crack-dealing days, was credited with reviving the East Coast scene (thus rivaling the West Coast) in 1994 on the Bad Boy label, which was launched in 1993 by Puffy Combs, a 22-year-old college-educated entrepreneur.

According to the Recording Industry Association of America (RIAA), rap music accounted for nearly 10% of total record sales in 1996, amounting to $1.1 billion. Industry statistics indicate Death Row Records alone generated $100 million; its hard-core recordings by Tupac Shakur and Snoop Doggy Dog ranked as the most successful. Bad Boy sold about $75 million worth of albums in 1996 from such artists as B.I.G., Faith Evans, Craig Mack, and 112.

Early on, Combs developed a reputation for cockiness

and arrogance, and Suge Knight developed a strong dislike for him. After Tupac joined Death Row, he too openly criticized Bad Boy, particularly Biggie Smalls. And Tupac fanned the flames with his public pronouncements on rap.

In Tupac's own estimation, no one could rap like Tupac could.

"Nobody can talk about pain like Tupac," he told *Vibe* magazine. "No one knows it like me. It separates me from other rappers. All the pain I'm talking about in my rap, you can see it." Tupac prided himself in embodying the thug-life aspect of gangsta rap.

When asked why he adopted the thug persona, he said, "Because if I don't, I'll lose everything I have. Who else is going to love me but the thugs?"

Tupac knew that the harder lyrics sold the most records, and that's what he continued to rap about. Besides "THUG LIFE" etched across his torso, Tupac also had the word "OUTLAW" tattooed on his arm. But writer Kevin Powell said being an outlaw in music was nothing new. White or black.

"In black culture, the outlaw figure has always existed, beginning with Chuck Berry. Sometimes people will put on the persona. A lot of times 'Pac wasn't the person he was rapping about; he *became* it. A lot of people in this generation have an 'I don't give a fuck' attitude.

"Hip-hop music is really a reaction to the failures and the fallacies of the so-called civil rights movement. A lot of these people say, 'We can vote now, we can sit in the bus, in the restaurant, but we don't own the bus, we don't own the restaurant.' So we say, 'Fuck it.' That's why you see a lot of people, white or black, frustrated. White kids are alienated too. They identify with rap and the hip-hop culture. It is the most cutting edge, most aggressive music out there. It's very rebellious. Historically, white youth have always identified with cultures that were rebellious. Tupac, to me, like Kurt Cobain [the grunge rocker who committed suicide], represented the bleak outlook on life that this generation, our generation, feels.

"I definitely understand why all these records are being sold. It's like the sixties, except there's no political movement. It's like an anarchy. A bunch of young people—black, white, straight, gay—it's like an individual revolt. I think 'Pac, more so than anybody, represented that individual revolt. Look at him—on one hand Tupac was this superstar, but on the other hand he was another young black man in jail."

Americans have long been fascinated with the connection between criminal life and pop culture—Frank Sinatra and his alleged mobster pals, for example, were immortalized in the *Godfather* saga. Gangsta rap, however, focuses on the young black male segment of society that has historically been ravaged by crime. Gangsta rap has been described as a form of release for those living in the ghetto, imprisoned in their own culture. Still, it's mostly the young white people from the suburbs who buy this music.

"Beneath all the ethnic specificity, these rappers are really imitating the lifestyle of white gangsters," the Reverend Jesse Jackson said after Tupac and Biggie were killed. "They have chosen white role models."

On the other hand, according to Las Vegas police, rappers and gangs aren't organized enough to imitate the real mob.

"Gangs are considered disorganized-organized crime," Sergeant Kevin Manning said. "[The Mafia] has a hierarchy. It's very organized. Everybody knows who reports to whom. It's not that way with gangs. They're organized in their own way. It's very fleeting. Everything they do seems random, but they are very powerful and violent."

Metro Sergeant Bill Keeton, who worked for eleven years in Metro's organized crime unit, says that the violence rap singers bring with them from the streets "is a cultural thing."

"Even though they make a lot of money, you can take the kid out of the street, but you can't take the street out of the kid. It's not organized crime. They're brought up around armed robberies, [and] they're pulling guns on each other."

Manning agreed, "These guys come up from the streets

and make millions of dollars. You've got somebody with a [gang] mentality who has a talent, but he can't handle it."

"Is the hip-hop generation all about violence and degradation?" CNN commentator Farai Chideya asked in a *Time* magazine piece. "Are we collectively doomed to go the way of Tupac Shakur and Biggie Smalls? I hope not, because I'm a member of that generation. In the weeks to come, as we try to make sense of the death of two of the youngest, richest, best-known black men in America, we'll probably succumb to a natural temptation to divide the 'good kids' from the 'hip-hop kids.' I'm not buying it. I grew up listening to hip-hop. In elementary school I tuned my radio to the techno-influenced chant of 'Planet Rock' and innocent party jams like 'Rappers Delight.' By high school and college, hip-hop was everything from the pop female braggadocio of Salt-n-Pepa to the black nationalism of Public Enemy. Today, in addition to music that ranges from alternative rock to techno, I listen to rough-edged rappers [like] the Wu Tang Clan—and, yes, Biggie and Tupac as well...

"Who's pushing the rawest rhymes to No. 1 on the charts? For years now, the largest volume of hip-hop albums has been sold to white suburban kids who've deposed heavy metal and elevated hip hop to the crown of Music Most Likely to Infuriate My Parents. The suburban rebellion—its record-buying tastes, its voyeurism of what too often it views as 'authentic black culture'—has contributed to the primacy of the gangsta-rap genre.

"The music may be in white America's homes, but the violence is in black America's neighborhoods. That's why we, the hip-hop generation, bear the ultimate responsibility for reshaping the art form we love. Hip hop used to lift us above the struggles we faced; then it tried to inform us about the struggles we faced; now it's *become* one of the struggles we face. I used to tell myself that the 'thug life' portrayed in the music was just fiction. Now it's incontrovertible fact. We can do better than this. If we don't, we're little more than voyeurs of our own demise."

• • •

While the murders of Tupac and Biggie spurred record sales, the long-term effects aren't good for business. The big record companies and distributors are asking themselves whether business should continue as usual. The music industry has weathered a storm of criticism for backing gangsta rap and its violent lyrics, especially when those lyrics are becoming more and more of a self-fulfilling prophesy. Some industry executives are wondering if it's ethical to be in business with unsavory characters with questionable backgrounds, in order to cash in on the lucrative market of gangsta rap record sales. The financial stakes are high, and the answers are somewhat contradictory. In order to survive, the hip-hop music industry needs to turn its bad-boy image around, while also maintaining its street authenticity.

When Senator Robert Dole, an outspoken moral crusader, singled out Death Row for producing CDs with lyrics that were unfit for the youth of America, Time Warner, Death Row's distributor, severed its ties with the label.

The white corporate world of the record industry is what Suge Knight, Puffy Combs, and other black record producers had to penetrate to get their rappers into the mainstream. One rap insider described Puffy and Suge as "middle men, liaisons between corporate America and black rappers."

But, according to other insiders, the bloodshed has alarmed the corporate bigwigs who have backed the rap record labels, so much that they're taking a harder look at who's being allowed to run their labels. "There is an uneasiness with gangsta rap even among the black executives and artists," the *New York Times* wrote in a feature about rap published before Tupac was killed.

That sentiment has been enhanced by the recent escalation in violence. On the heels of the murders of Tupac Shakur and Biggie Smalls, some prominent industry executives are privately questioning whether greed is blinding record companies to the increasing body count now attributed to gangsta rap. A decision to tone down the music would be a major one, with enormous financial ramifications. It could mean less money for the companies, but it could also translate to saving lives. The beat could go on, but a little softer.

Death Row and Suge Knight have lost Tupac Shakur; Bad Boy and Puffy Combs have lost Biggie Smalls. The future is uncertain for the heads of the two top rap labels. Suge is in prison. Puffy is free but frightened.

As the Death Row battleship sinks into an ocean of bad publicity and management, some of its stalwarts seem to have seen the writing on the wall and are abandoning ship. In 1996 before Tupac was killed, Dr. Dre split acrimoniously with Death Row, telling the *Hollywood Reporter* only days before Shakur's shooting, 'Gangsta rap is definitely a thing of the past. I've just moved on.'"

Meanwhile, federal investigators have been building a racketeering case against Death Row Records by probing alleged links to street gangs, drug traffickers, and organized crime figures, sources told the *Los Angeles Times*.

Investigators believe Death Row may have been bankrolled by the notorious Bloods street gang and East Coast organized crime figures. The investigation involves agents from the FBI, the Internal Revenue Service, the Bureau of Alcohol, Tobacco and Firearms, and the Drug Enforcement Administration. Police in Los Angeles and Las Vegas are also reportedly working on the case.

According to the *Los Angeles Times*, federal investigators are determining if members of the Bloods committed crimes while on Death Row's payroll, and whether Death Row was launched with drug money or other illegal funds. Suge's association with convicted drug kingpins Michael "Harry O" Harris and Ricardo Crockett, both of whom are now in prison, is also being looked at by federal agents. Suge says he knew the men, but did not take money from them to launch his company. The feds believe Harris may have helped bankroll Death Row. And because Harris is serving time for, among other things, a drug conviction, they believe drug money may have been used.

According to a federal grand jury indictment filed in Las Vegas in 1993, Suge Knight was listed as the 34th defendant, along with Crockett, in a drug-distribution ring in which cocaine was brought in from Los Angeles and sold in Las Vegas. The indictment alleged that Crockett ran the operation, selling the cocaine to his sub-distributors for further sale in the Las Vegas area between July 1992 and May 1993. The indictment also charged that Crockett and others used guns to protect the operation or to rob other drug dealers of money and drugs. Suge ended up with a gun-possession conviction and received probation. Crockett was convicted of drug charges and remains in prison.

The feds are also reportedly looking at Suge's investment in the now-defunct Club 662 for links to organized crime. On February 13, 1997, a federal grand jury subpoenaed the financial records of Suge, his attorney David Kenner, Death Row Records, and 36 companies, including Club 662, and individuals who have done business with them.

One of Suge's many lawyers is John Spilotro, attorney of record for the 1987 attempted murder charge in Las Vegas. He's the son of the late Chicago mobster Anthony "Tony the Ant" Spilotro, said to be an "enforcer" and the muscle behind the mob in Las Vegas in the 1970s.

Suge vehemently denied the federal allegations of ties to organized crime, from L.A. County Jail where he was incarcerated at the time, claiming he was being targeted because of his race. "This is the most outrageous story I have ever heard," he told the *L.A. Times*. "A black brother from Compton creates a company that helps people in the ghetto, so what does the government do? They try to bring him down."

Suge's attorney, David Kenner, also strongly denied allegations of mob ties to the New York Genovese family, telling reporters, "Suge wouldn't know a member of the Genovese crime family if he tripped over him."

Oscar Goodman, a notorious Las Vegas attorney who has

made a successful career of representing mob figures, went to Los Angeles during one of Suge's probation hearings as a consultant on the case. Now he waits in the wings, ready to represent Suge Knight should the feds bring an indictment down on Suge or Death Row. Goodman is a partner with David Chesnoff, one of three attorneys who escorted Suge to homicide when he was questioned about Tupac's murder.

"I went down to Los Angeles as a consultant on [Suge's] revocation case," Goodman said. "I went down there for one court proceeding and counseled with the lawyers who actually made the presentation. The judge [Superior Court Judge Stephen Czuleger], in my opinion, went through the charade of pretending to afford Knight due process and gave the decision. The presentation by defense attorneys couldn't have been better. They walked beautifully through their presentation to the judge. They shouldn't have wasted their time and effort. The judge, I think, enjoyed the media attention, and it was a foregone decision. It was a done deal. Before they even made their presentation, the judge's mind was already made up, the decision was made, and the judgment typed up.

"On the federal case, if there ever was any federal case, if anything ever came to light federally, I would probably be involved," Goodman predicted.

In a standard FBI-style statement, Special Agent John Hoose with the FBI's Los Angeles bureau said, "We've neither confirmed nor denied there's an investigation." End of conversation.

But George Kelesis, another Las Vegas attorney who has represented Suge, said he got a call from out-of-state FBI agents after Tupac was shot in Las Vegas, questioning him about Suge's business dealings. He said he believes the feds have targeted Suge unfairly.

"He was definitely a target," Kelesis said. "I think it has more to do with the image, the image that they manifest. I can tell you I have not seen a shred of any tangible evidence that would indicate to me that he is involved in a criminal enterprise. And I'm not blowing smoke and hot air."

• • •

Tupac's record label made an attempt to cash in on his death by trying to sell the car in which he was shot. After learning that Primadonna Resorts in Primm, Nevada had purchased the bullet-riddled car in which Bonnie and Clyde Barrow were killed in a 1934 shootout, a representative from Death Row contacted the casino company. Aaron Cohen, a spokesman for the resort, said they weren't interested in buying the car.

Cohen explained, "It's not a piece of American history the way the Bonnie and Clyde car is. Maybe in 20 years it will be."

Likewise, the bullet-riddled door of the rented GMC Suburban in which Notorious B.I.G. was gunned down is getting ready to go on the auction block, but to raise money for charity, not for Biggie's record company. The passenger door was the only portion of the GMC that was damaged in the shooting. The rental company that owns it plans to auction it off for around $3,000 or $4,000, a spokesman said.

On top of everything else, on January 7, 1996, Suge, David Kenner, and Death Row were sued in Los Angeles Superior Court by American Express Travel Related Services. American Express claimed that Suge, Kenner, Kenner's wife Erica, and Death Row Records owed the credit-card company upwards of $1.5 million. American Express alleged a breach of contract and sought payment in full, plus court costs, attorney fees, and prejudgment interest.

The court documents itemize Death Row's expenses, including those charged while Tupac Shakur lay in a coma at University Medical Center, a paper trail that leads to limousine services, pricey hotel rooms, and private planes.

Kenner held both gold and platinum American Express accounts. Erica Kenner was also a signatory on one of the cards. Suge and Death Row employees were authorized to make charges on the platinum account, but only with Kenner's approval, the *New Times* in Los Angeles reported.

American Express stated in its suit that "all parties had customarily used and paid for charges before October 1996 on Kenner's cards with no objections." Kenner paid for his and his wife's expenses "regularly and promptly," the credit card company said. Death Row debts were paid for with checks from Death Row's corporate account, which was administered by Kenner, the newspaper *New Times* learned from a civil suit against Suge filed by Dr. Dre.

Kenner told the *Los Angeles Times* that the disputed charges "were put on these cards without the authorization of Mr. Knight or myself for expenditures that had nothing to do with us."

Some of the charges, however, included fight tickets for the Tyson-Seldon match on September 7. The American Express bills were sent directly to Kenner's Encino, California, law offices, the *New Times* reported.

Thirteen pages in the suit itemized the expenses charged from June to September 1996.

Kenner's wife charged $3,763.69 to Dial-a-Mattress, Bed Bad & Beyond, Nobody Beats the Wiz, and the NYU Book Center in New York, and Ralph Lauren and Barey's in Beverly Hills. Also included was airfare to New York City. These charges appear to be personal and household items to outfit Erica Kenner and her home at the expense of Death Row Records.

Las Vegas-related expenses included chartered jets—at a cost of $42,279.86—from Jetwest International on September 4 and September 17, plus jet refuel charges of $23,042.88 from Spirit Aviation. Kenner also reportedly charged airfare of $122,303.44 to Bel Aire Travel. On September 19 there was another Bel Aire Travel charge of $108,294.95. (A cellular telephone recording answers for Bel Aire Travel.) Limousine services were charged to CLS Transportation on September 12 and September 13 for $160,000.

The records also show that Suge booked 27 separate hotel rooms at the Luxor Hotel at $50 per night (or $1,584.21) and spent $666.45 at the Tinder Box in Las Vegas. A charge on September 12 was made to CLS Transportation for $50,000. A charge on September 21 was made at the Beverly Hills Hotel for $2,738.82. Besides the actual expenses, American Express had tacked on an additional $25,787.43 late fee.

A Luxor Hotel spokesman, who asked not to be identified, said that only two hotel rooms were booked by Suge Knight that week, and that Knight had been billed only for the two rooms.

In perhaps the strangest turn of events, Suge was accused by a former accountant for Death Row Records of assaulting him, in what *The Wall Street Journal* termed a "horrifying encounter."

On the morning of Saturday, October 12, 1996, Coopers & Lybrand accountant Steven Cantrock told his boss that he had attended a meeting with Suge Knight the night before and claimed that Suge had "assaulted him, forced him to his knees, and made him sign a trumped-up IOU," the newspaper reported.

In the IOU, Cantrock confessed that he had stolen $4.5 million from his client, Suge Knight.

"The coerced statement, he assured his shocked Coopers associates, was false and absurd," *The Wall Street Journal's* Alix M. Freedman and Laurie P. Cohen wrote.

Troubling questions soon emerged, and Cantrock eventually left the firm with his story in doubt. Coopers declined to comment to *The Wall Street Journal*, other than to say that it had "severed ties with both accountant and client."

Coopers' association with Death Row began in November 1992, when Cantrock landed the account with the record label, which had been looking for someone to manage the financial end of its business. Cantrock was given sole authority to write checks for the rap label.

"Mr. Knight and his roving entourage were huge spend-ers, even by Hollywood standards," the newspaper reported. "Rather than rein them in, Mr. Cantrock went with the flow...When the Death Row clan was on the road, Mr. Cantrock saw to it that stretch limousines were lined up outside their hotels 24 hours a day, as Mr. Knight desired. The accountant signed off on their impulse purchases of Rolex watches, Lexus cars, yachts, and jewelry."

One thing Cantrock wasn't able to accomplish, however, was organizing Death Row's financial affairs; the rap label was perpetually short of cash.

Suge told *The Wall Street Journal*, through his attorney, that he "was in the dark" about money problems and believed "everything was fine."

Suge began to realize there was a problem when Cantrock started to lose clients at Coopers & Lybrand. Suge began paying more attention, and he quickly suspected that Death Row funds were missing. He confronted Cantrock for the first time on June 4, 1996, the newspaper reported, asking him about the missing money, including a refund of $25,000 for the down payment on a Las Vegas house Suge had decided not to purchase. Cantrock reportedly admitted taking the money. Suge told him, "Just stop stealing, pay me back, and get on the ball with putting the business in order."

But by June 1996, Death Row's financial situation was already a shambles. Suge claimed he wasn't getting an accounting of the books from Cantrock and was still kept completely in the dark. So Suge called a meeting at a San Fernando Valley home attended by several people, including his attorney David Kenner. An IOU was written and signed by Cantrock. Those present in the room during the confrontation disputed Cantrock's claim that he signed it under duress.

On February 7, 1997, Coopers issued a statement that it had "asked for and received [Cantrock's] resignation" for violating the firm's policies.

Death Row Records hasn't tried to collect the $4.5 million it says it's owed, although Kenner has said he is contemplating a lawsuit against Cantrock and Coopers & Lybrand.

10

RAP VIOLENCE, GANG VIOLENCE

Since November 30, 1994, the day Tupac Shakur was shot in the lobby of Quad Studios in Manhattan, there have been five murders of people directly involved in the rap-music business: Tupac, Randy Walker, Yafeu Fula, Jake Robles, and Biggie Smalls. In addition, at least another dozen people known to be affiliated with the Bloods and Crips gangs have been wounded or killed in drive-by shootings. In most of the cases, homicide and gang detectives involved in the investigations say the assaults and murders aren't connected.

People in the music industry think otherwise. Many people in the rap-music industry are worried, wondering who's next.

Snoop Doggy Dogg, a rapper for Death Row Records, postponed a music tour a week after Biggie Smalls was killed. Snoop delayed the Lollapalooza tour for a month, he said, out of respect for Biggie, but others say it was out of fear. Indeed, he rented an armored bullet-proof vehicle (said to be equipped with holes for weapons) instead of riding the bus with the crew.

"Tupac has been killed, and six months later [Biggie was] killed, and he doesn't want to be next," Jeff Bowen, booking and marketing director at Winston-Salem's (North Carolina)

Lawrence Joel Veterans Memorial Coliseum, told The Associated Press. Bowen said Snoop was expected to begin his tour—the Doggfather East-West Fresh Fest 1997 World Tour—sometime in April 1997. His revamped tour was to include a film tribute to Biggie and Tupac. Instead of opening in Winston-Salem, it opened May 1 in San Diego, closer to Snoop's L.A. base, and included the film tribute for his slain fellow rappers.

"Snoop is the only one left," J. Howell, owner of C&J Concert Promotions, told a reporter. "He will take it to the forefront and let people—let kids—know that it's not all about [violence]. He's coming out with a band and talking about peace and unity, whether you're white, black, green, or yellow."

Snoop Doggy Dog wasn't the only one who was scared off. Warren G's record-company executives postponed a promotional tour for his new album, *Take a Look Over Your Shoulder*, because they feared for his safety.

Havoc, a rapper with the band Mobb Deep, told reporter David Bauder that the violence can't be ignored.

"We're walking targets because we're rappers, we're entertainers. We've got to be careful," he said.

Ice T agreed, telling Bauder, "This is the first time I ever felt unsafe."

Luke, a rapper formerly with the band 2 Live Crew, said many rappers were nervous. "It's unsafe for Snoop to come to a concert in New York, for Nas to go to a concert in L.A., because there ain't nobody finding these people who are killing everybody."

On June 28, 1997, Snoop Doggy Dogg attended the Evander Holyfield-Mike Tyson rematch heavyweight bout at the MGM Grand in Las Vegas. Witnesses claim that shots rang out inside the casino (Metro denies it). An ensuing stampede injured several dozen people, but Snoop escaped unscathed. He was seen being guarded by Nation of Islam security officers (who are easily identified by their bow ties).

• • •

On September 24, 1995, 10 months after Tupac was shot at Quad Studios, Jake Robles, a close friend of Suge and an employee of Death Row, was shot at an Atlanta nightclub. Robles died a week later. Suge blamed Puffy Combs and Bad Boy Entertainment's associates for the shooting.

Then, on November 30, 1995, a year to the day after the first attempt on Tupac's life, a key witness to that shooting was murdered. Randy "Stretch" Walker, a close friend of Tupac, was shot by three assailants during a high-speed chase in Queens. As with most of the other "unrelated" murder cases involving gangsta rappers, Walker's killer (or killers) remains at large.

After the April 1996 Soul Train Awards, someone pulled a gun when associates with Bad Boy Entertainment and Death Row Records exchanged heated words in the parking lot.

On July 3, 1996, Biggie Smalls, Li'l Caesar (of Junior M.A.F.I.A.), Lil' Kim, and DJ Enuff narrowly escaped a possible hit attempt, the *Village Voice* reported. Biggie had gone to Atlanta to represent Puffy Combs and Bad Boy Entertainment at a concert. But during his set, Tupac's crew began taunting Biggie and shouting "Tupac! Tupac! Tupac!"

Afterward, Biggie and his crew were followed to their hotel by people in a van they believed were trying to kill them. With the crews' Glock 9-millimeters locked and cocked, one of Biggie's bodyguards told the *Voice*, Biggie's vehicle made a series of radical maneuvers leading to the interstate. The people following them apparently realized "they'd been made," the guard said, then pulled in front of Biggie's vehicle. Biggie's crew thought they might have to shoot their way out of it.

"Face it," the bodyguard told the *Voice*. "There wasn't no questions gonna be asked. You knew it was on and what you had to do right then."

The van and a truck continued shadowing them as they

drove on the interstate and around the suburbs of Atlanta.

Biggie, the bodyguard said, wanted to find out who they were. "Pull over and see what they want," he told the driver. They did—and the truck and van sped off. Biggie and his entourage returned to the hotel without learning the identities of the people in the van.

"The next day we found out that Tupac did come into town that night and he stayed in the hotel across the street from where Biggie was staying, and he left that morning," the bodyguard told the *Voice*.

Then Tupac and Biggie were killed in drive-by shootings and Yafeu Fula was executed gangland-style. The alleged killers of Yafeu Fula have been arrested, but till now, the gunmen who killed Tupac, Biggie, Robles, and Walker have gotten away with murder.

One thing police don't dispute is that all the shootings have been executed in gang-style high-caliber drive-bys.

But as for police claims that these murders were all unrelated, it's a difficult sell. It was common knowledge that Randy Walker was a witness in the November 30, 1994, shooting of Tupac in Manhattan. Tupac and others said they believed Walker was murdered because of that, and that his death was not random. Many in the music industry feel the same way about Yafeu Fula's death. He was a witness to Tupac's fatal shooting, so he, too, had to be executed, to eliminate the possibility that he'd drop a dime and talk. Then, when Biggie Smalls was murdered in a scenario similar to Tupac's, talk that it was retaliation for Shakur's shooting spread. Still, police from coast to coast have been hesitant to say any of the killings are related. At this point, it's anyone's guess as to whether the murder connections, if any, are real or perceived. Could they be, as the police have suggested, just gang-bangers doing their thing, in random shootings, coincidentally hitting witnesses to other murders?

• • •

If the murders of Jake Robles, Randy "Stretch" Walker, Tupac Shakur, Yafeu Fula, and Biggie Smalls are gang-related, the fatal results of a war between the Bloods and Crips, people in the gangsta-rap business say they won't be the last.

In the past, gang members carried Saturday Night Specials. Today's black gangs are armed with sophisticated paramilitary weapons such as semiautomatic rifles, Uzis, Mach-10-type firearms, and 9-millimeter and .45-caliber pistols.

There are several stories about the origins of the Crips, but the most commonly accepted version is that the gang was started in the neighborhoods of West Los Angeles. The smaller neighborhood gangs consolidated and joined forces, forming the larger, and more powerful, Crips gang. An influential gang member named Raymond Washington started the Crips, which gradually built a reputation for being the strongest force among the black gangs of West L.A. Soon, other gangs started renaming themselves, incorporating the word Crips into their new names; gangs such as the Main Street Crips, Kitchen Crips, 5 Deuce Crips, and Rollin 20 Crips appeared.

The development of the Bloods has been similar to that of the Crips. Black men in their late teens and early 20s living in rival neighborhoods in Compton formed the Bloods. In the early '70s Sylvester Scott and Vincent Owens formed the Compton Pirus, named for West Piru Street in the city of Compton. The Compton Pirus rose to power quickly and became extremely powerful. As the recognition given to the Compton Pirus spread throughout L.A. County, other Pirus gangs, which later changed their name to Bloods, were formed. Today, the Bloods are the most formidable rivals of the Crips.

Numerically, the Bloods are outnumbered by the Crips, according to Compton and Los Angeles police. But what the Bloods lack in numbers, they make up for in violence.

Sometime in the early '70s, police began to notice that

the black gangs were dividing into Crips and Bloods. But though many of the gangs fall under the loose umbrella defined by the two best-known names, the smaller sets are still identified by the local streets, landmarks, parks, or neighborhoods, which are incorporated into their names—the Donna Street gang in North Las Vegas, for example, and the 18th Street gang in Las Vegas. Today, Crips often have altercations among their own subsets or factions. Bloods, on the other hand, don't seem so inclined.

In the Compton area, police have seen different Crips gangs unite to enhance their criminal enterprises. The Crips gangs began calling themselves C.C. Riders (Compton Crips Riders). They've spread to other Western states, including Nevada.

(In the late 1980s, southern California gang members began traveling into Las Vegas, one of the hottest spots in the nation and, to the gangs, a ready mark. The gangs had a similar M.O.: takeover robberies of banks and casinos. Gang members considered casinos, especially, an easy score according to gang-unit detectives. They were able to grab a large sum of money in just a couple of minutes. When casinos were hit, some of the money was later found by Los Angeles area police in gang sweeps. The disturbing thing for officers, however, was that the takeover robberies seemed to serve as an initiation ritual for new Los Angeles-based gang members. The police swooped in on the early perpetrators and slowed the practice down a bit. But they couldn't stop it completely.)

Crips gang members identify with the color blue, and usually have a blue rag in their possession or wear some blue article of clothing (such as blue shoelaces, blue hat, blue hair rollers, blue canvas belts). They generally write their graffiti in blue, tagging their gang name on walls in the 'hoods to mark their territorial boundaries and to publicly taunt their enemies or rivals. They use terms like "Crip," or "BK" or PK" (which means Blood Killer or Piru Killer). Crips refer to one another as "Cuzz" and use the letter "C" to replace the letter "B" in their conversations and writings, such as "Meet me at the cusstop," and "That guy has crass calls."

Pirus and Bloods identify with the color red and refer to one another as "Blood." A Piru usually carries a red rag and wears red clothing. Bloods gangs write their graffiti in red and use the terms "Piru" and "CK" (for Crips Killer).

Black gang members once eschewed tattoos, but that's changed; now black gang members are tattooing themselves in the same manner as the traditional Hispanic gangs.

In the black street gang, there is little structure in terms of hierarchy and rank. No one member is in charge of everyone. Some members have more influence than others, but the term "leader" is seldom used. A person's age, physical stature, arrest record, and behavioral background are the main factors that determine an individual's influence upon a gang. Gang members gain respect, influence, and power within a particular gang by demonstrating their nerve and daring.

Each gang's level of violence is determined by the dominant members' ability to incite the others. The dominant members are generally the most violent, street-wise, and knowledgeable in legal matters, which is especially useful in the event their members are arrested. They might participate in a violent act, or simply encourage others to commit it. They're usually well liked and respected by their fellow gang members, as well as by outsiders.

Are black gangs becoming the new mob? Claims of "disorganization" not withstanding, some cops think so. Police claim that black gangs and the mob now overlap, with players from organized crime hiring gang members as their hit men.

"I compare [black gang members] to the early days of the mob," said North Las Vegas Police Lt. Chris Larotonda. "They're doing the exact same things. Then it was bootleg whiskey. Now it's drugs. But you have to make yourself look legitimate even though your money may be coming from other [illegal] sources. Some of the gangs are expanding in just the narcotics sales and [otherwise] trying to legitimize themselves. We've seen them try to branch out into more legitimate-type businesses."

Even U.S. Senator Harry Reid, D-Nev., has likened Nevada's street gang members to mobsters. Reid told a Judiciary Committee considering an anti-gang measure that "we've got sophisticated crime syndicates turning our cities and towns into war zones."

The basic difference between traditional organized crime versus street gangs "[usually comes down to] access to political influence," said Lt. Bill Conger from Metro's gang unit. "The street gangs aren't organized enough for that, yet."

Black street gangs are alive and well in Las Vegas. Although L.A. gangs influenced them, they now stand alone.

"We have our own Crips and Bloods," said Conger. "There was some Los Angeles influence early on, but Las Vegas is its own town, and we have our own [gang] problems."

11

MOTIVES

There are several.

According to police sources and talk on the street, the killing of Tupac Shakur (and, to an extent, Biggie Smalls) was a by-product of one of three pre-existing situations: one, the fierce competition between East Coast and West Coast music factions to sell records and dominate the gangsta rap world; two, Tupac Shakur's and Suge Knight's connections to the street gang the Bloods and its rivalry with the Crips; and three, a conspiracy of top record-company executives to kill their own superstar rappers as a way of boosting sales.

Each of these three theories has also spawned related sub-theories. One relating to the third scenario is that Suge Knight was behind the deed (an accusation that Knight vehemently denies). Conversely, it has been suggested that Suge, not Tupac, was the intended victim.

Still, others who have followed this saga contend that it was nothing so sinister as a deep-rooted conspiracy, but more likely a case of personal retaliation (stemming from the fight at the MGM), or a semi-random act of violence, *semi*-random to the extent that the rival-gang consideration would be involved if this were the case.

One music industry insider said, "The only scenario that

fits is somebody thought they were doing 'Pac a favor [by killing Biggie]. I don't know who killed Tupac. I'm tired of the speculation."

Tupac himself has been named in speculation that there really was no killing; that the whole thing was an elaborate dodge staged to fake his death. (This theory is discussed in the next chapter.)

Let's take a look.

"R-E-S-P-E-C-T," Aretha Franklin sang 20 years ago. And that's what Suge Knight, Tupac Shakur, Biggie Smalls, and Puffy Combs all said was what they wanted today. Could the vicious and bloody rivalry between record companies be as simple as that?

Some sources say that the rivalry has indeed been as simple as that—respect as rappers and songwriters, as businessmen, and as gangstas.

"The rumors [about a feud] are helpful, but not true," Suge told *Vibe* before Tupac was killed. "They get me additional respect, and this business is about getting the respect you deserve so you can get what you want. I don't worry about all the talk."

Tupac also spoke to *Vibe* about being respected for his music, while at the same time appearing to be willing to fight Suge's East Coast battles with him.

"My homeboy Suge gave me the best advice that I could ever get from anybody," Tupac said. "When people ask Suge if he's beefing with Bad Boy and Puffy, he says, 'It's like me goin' to the playground to pick on little kids. That's like me being mad at my little brother 'cause he's getting cash now. I'm not mad at that; I'm just mad at my little brother when he don't respect me. And when you don't respect me, I'm a spank that ass. I don't give a fuck how rich you got on the block, I'm your big brother. That's my only point. I feel as though he wrong, he got out of hand. He got seduced by the power—

not because he's an evil person, but because money is evil if it's not handled right.'"

"Why is it mandatory that I get respect?" Tupac said to writer William Shaw. "I know other people who are just as successful as me and you can call *them* a bitch...but if somebody calls me a bitch, I don't care if we're in court, we're going to fight." In his world, he told Shaw, "All good niggers, all the niggers who change the world, die in violence. They don't die in regular ways. Motherfuckers come take their lives."

Some observers maintain, however, that the bicoastal feud was more about money and women than personalities, that it was these tangible status symbols that led to the professional jealousies.

Producer Jermaine Dupree, a friend of Puffy Combs, told *Newsweek*: "This industry has a problem with people thinking there isn't enough room for everyone. It's the attitude that, 'If you got it, I can't have it, so I am going to take it.' That's why these deaths are happening."

But of course, the rivalry motive is far more involved than that. Deep down, Tupac wondered if Biggie really had set him up to get robbed and shot at Quad Studios in 1994. Though he occasionally denied it, Tupac told San Francisco deejay Sway two months before he was killed, "Strangers, niggahs in jail told me, 'Hell, you don't know who shot you? Biggie's homeboys shot you.'"

"Tupac really believes Biggie and them shot him," veteran rapper Ice-T said in a *Vibe* magazine interview. "If somebody thinks they shot them, it's on for life."

When Tupac signed with Death Row, he began publicly attacking Biggie, even bragging that he'd had sex with Biggie's wife Faith Evans. Then in 1996 at the Soul Train Awards in Los Angeles, Biggie's armed bodyguard got into a fight with an armed associate of Tupac backstage at the Shrine Auditorium. That's when the rivalry started being referred to as an East Coast-West Coast rap war.

On the other hand, Tupac's cousin, Chaka Zulu, told a

reporter, "I don't think [the feud] came out of 'Pac's camp. I think it came from people that are caught up in the hype of the East Coast-West Coast thing."

For his part, Biggie and his friends vociferously denied it. Lance "Un" Rivera, Biggie's partner in the Brooklyn record-label management company Undeas Recording, said in a published interview that the accusations were unfounded.

"He and Tupac didn't have no beef," Rivera told *Rolling Stone* magazine. "They was real close friends. Tupac developed a hate for him. [Biggie] couldn't understand what it was, but he never responded. He said, 'I'm not going to feed into it.'"

Biggie, in his last interview, published in *The Source* the week after he died, again insisted the rift between him and Tupac was blown out of proportion. But no one has ever said whether Biggie had an alibi for either—or both—the Manhattan and the Las Vegas shootings of Tupac. When asked, the police said they didn't know, because Biggie was never a suspect.

The rivalry wasn't relegated to Tupac and Biggie. It went right to the top. Suge Knight's Death Row Records had been battling Puffy Combs' Bad Boy Entertainment for control of the multimillion-dollar rap music industry for a few years, and the rivalry heightened further, some say, after the 1995 Source Awards in August at the Paramount Theater in Manhattan, when Suge criticized Combs on stage, making fun of his appearances on videos with Bad Boy artists. Suge was an award presenter. Before he left the stage, he said, "If you don't want the owner of your label on your album or in your video or on your tour, come sign with Death Row."

This was an obvious shot at Combs, who occasionally appears in his rappers' videos and sometimes raps on their albums. Puffy was shocked by Suge's blatant and public disrespect, and some say a battle to the death began that night. A few months later at a party for producer Jermaine Dupree, a Death Row employee and Suge's close friend Jake Robles was shot. When he died a week later, Suge blamed Puffy

Combs, calling it a hit. No one was ever arrested and Puffy has denied any involvement.

Movie actor Warren Beatty became friendly with Suge while researching a movie project set in the rap world. Beatty dismissed talk that Suge would retaliate against Puffy for Jake's death.

"It's sort of hard to keep up with the apocryphal on Suge," Beatty told the *New York Times*. "I mean, Puff Daddy, Muff Daddy, whatever. I know Suge was very close to the man who died. And I know he was very upset. The apocryphal is just talk, even when it's pungent."

Still, rumors persisted, and if they had any substance, the feud had escalated. Now people were being marked for death. What may have started out as hype to sell records had turned violent.

Steve Jackson, a rap music producer who was with Biggie the night he was killed, told the *Village Voice*, "You know as well as I know that people wanna avenge Biggie's death, man, because they are very sad over the fact that he was set up. They have friends and their friends have friends and their friends want revenge. You still have Suge Knight, you still have Puffy Combs, you still have their friends. You still have the East, you still have the West."

"Now everybody is scared," Jackson continued. "I don't think it would be in the best interest of Puffy to go back to L.A. any time in the future. I don't think he should go back, period. I think they're definitely going to try to kill him. Somebody is out to kill him, just as they killed Biggie Smalls."

"It's a war that neither Death Row nor Bad Boy can contain," *Village Voice* reporter Peter Noel wrote on March 25, 1997. "Combs, Knight, and Snoop Doggy Dogg are undoubtedly concerned for their own lives."

"What you have are two of our biggest stars killed—shot down—within six months," said Dominique DiPrima, a deejay at L.A.'s KKBT. "This is out of control."

• • •

While the East-West record-label rivalry was a prevalent early theory for a motive in the shooting, many blamed another, more obvious, rivalry: the ongoing battle between the Bloods and Crips street gangs. In the days immediately following the shooting, rumors ran rampant that Tupac took a bullet meant for Suge, and that Tupac died in a war that involved gang members from Suge's old Compton neighborhood. *Vibe* Editor-in-Chief, Alan Light, said "[I] wouldn't be surprised if it didn't have anything to do with Tupac, but is more related to Suge. There have been up to three contracts on [Suge's] life at any given moment. He's very public...about his gang affiliation. There are a lot of people with a lot of issues with him."

In a photo taken just minutes before Tupac was shot, Suge is pictured holding a blood-red rag in his hand, a well-known sign of Bloods affiliation. Meanwhile, Orlando Anderson, who was beaten by Tupac's crew at the MGM Grand the night of his shooting, was a reputed member of the Southside Crips, according to Compton police.

According to a police affidavit, two months before Tupac was killed, there was a confrontation between some Crips and Bloods at the Lakewood Mall near Compton. Travon Lane, aka Tray Dee, a Mob Piru member and rap singer, was in the mall's Foot Locker store with Kevin Woods, also a known Piru, when they were confronted by about eight Southside Crips members. The two crews fought and Tray's diamond-laden Death Row pendant was stolen.

On September 7, Tray was in Las Vegas for the Tyson-Seldon fight with Suge, Tupac, and Death Row associates. After the boxing match, Tray reportedly recognized Orlando Anderson as one of the Crips who, he claimed, stole his pendant. Tupac, Suge, and the crew stomped and kicked Orlando, which was captured on the now-famous MGM Grand surveillance videotape. Police in the L.A. area were given this information from L.A. gang-member informants. Investigators won't say if they tracked down and interviewed Travon Lane (it's their policy not to release names of, or information about, witnesses).

Could Orlando have caught up with Suge and Tupac later that evening and taken his revenge? Did Orlando Anderson have an alibi at 11:10 p.m. on September 7? Las Vegas police won't say. "We usually don't comment on statements made by potential witnesses and suspects," Sergeant Kevin Manning said.

The random (or semi-random) theory supposes that rival gang members simply happened upon the Death Row caravan at Flamingo and Koval. And, finding themselves in a serendipitous position, perpetrated a spontaneous attack.

George Kelesis, the Las Vegas attorney who'd organized the benefit at Club 662 the night of the shooting, said, "I never really have reconciled it. I've heard so many stories...It could have been, in my mind, as simple as just some gang-banger trying to make a name for himself. The possibilities are infinite. To buy into the story that it was [planned], how in God's earth did they pull it off? Tupac drove in to Las Vegas at the last minute. Plans change.

"I was supposed to go in the limo with Suge, but people started lining up at Club 662 at 5 o'clock. I couldn't leave the benefit, so Suge went in [Tupac's] car. Everything that happened prior to the fight was all last minute. The plans were changed at the last minute and nobody, not even us, knew it. Suge was going to come late and a lot of stars were coming late. I think the shooting was happenstance. If it was a plan to kill him, then those guys were good because they had to have a crystal ball to figure it out."

In either the retaliation or the random scenarios, it's possible that it wasn't Tupac who was specifically targeted. Killing Tupac or Suge would have sufficed, and circumstances (the traffic pattern) resulted in Tupac's side of the car taking the brunt of the attack.

If nothing else, any version of the gang motive provides

an easy out for investigators. "In my opinion, it was black gang-related, probably a Bloods-Crips thing," Metro gang detective Chuck Cassell told Kevin Powell. "Look at [Tupac's] tattoos and album covers—that's not the Jackson 5...It looks like a case of live by the sword, die by the sword."

At the hospital the afternoon Tupac died, a woman who had been standing with Tupac's family, describing herself as a family friend, hinted that there would be retaliation for Tupac's death. "You're not going to hear any talk about retaliation here. That'll come later," she said to me as she stood inside the trauma center's lobby.

Marcos, a friend of Tupac who had met him on the set of a video 18 months earlier, sat on the hood of a white BMW parked outside the trauma center 30 minutes after Tupac was pronounced dead. Marcos was wearing a collarless, crisp white shirt and white shorts. A couple of his friends stood stoically beside him. They all had the "L.A. look" with their clothing style and jewelry. As Marcos began talking to reporters, his friends backed away.

When asked, "Why are you here?" Marcos looked down and answered quietly, "Man, to show my respect to Tupac. To show respect to his family and his mother. We're here for her. We're here for 'Pac."

After the reporters were done with Marcos, I stuck around and asked him if friends of Tupac knew who the assailant was. He said, "Yeah, we know. We know who did it."

Then I asked why, if they knew who the shooter was, didn't they tell the police? He replied, "Nobody wants to help the police. What for? What are they gonna do? They can't bring him back.

"I'm just saying that whoever did this is going to get found. The people who find him, I don't know what they'll do, but they'll take care of it in their own way."

When I asked if the assailants would eventually leak information that they shot Tupac, he said, "They already have." He declined to say who did it. All he'd say was, "They're not from Las Vegas."

• • •

Finally, could Suge have possibly ordered Tupac hit to sell more CDs? Some observers don't think it's as farfetched as it sounds. As one insider put it, "Think about it. Tupac's worth more dead than alive."

According to a police source, Suge Knight had been considered a possible suspect from the beginning, especially in light of rumors that a hefty life insurance policy had been taken out on Tupac before his death. According to the rumors, after Tupac signed with Death Row, a $4 million insurance policy was written on him, naming Death Row, not Tupac's family, the beneficiary.

Rick Fischbein, Afeni Shakur's attorney who represents Tupac's estate, said he, too, had heard talk about the insurance policy, but said, "We haven't been able to substantiate it."

Metro P.D.'s Sgt. Kevin Manning said that no one, including Suge Knight, had been eliminated as a potential suspect. But when asked what Knight could have gained financially with Tupac gone, Manning said, "I have no comment about the money."

A representative for the State of California's Office of Insurance said no claims of fraud and no investigations had been opened in the Shakur case. It's not known which company, if any, wrote the policy.

"Death is a commodity, you know?" commented Ramsey Jones, a clerk at Tower Records in Greenwich Village, New York, explaining to *The Associated Press* why he couldn't keep Biggie's CDs on the shelf (they were selling quicker than he could stock them).

A music-industry insider who asked not to be identified had this to say. "Here's my theory. [At first], these rap artists are small-time investments. They're lucky if they make one album. When they start getting up to four albums, they're big investments. Then they become a liability. [And they remain] a liability as long as they're alive. They lead lavish lifestyles and get in trouble. Tupac Shakur and Biggie Smalls, they got themselves in trouble a lot. They had big mouths. The record companies had to bail them out all the time, get them out of trouble. They had to keep throwing money at them for their lifestyles—their cars, their condos, their women.

"But if they're dead and they've already cut their albums, the record companies are just selling their albums. They're not giving the money to them any more. They don't cost them anything. The green keeps coming in but they don't have to spend anything to get it, you understand? Green comes in and nothing goes out to the rappers because they're dead."

At the time of his death, Tupac had some 200 songs recorded—worth potentially hundreds of millions of dollars. And by all accounts, he'd certainly taken on the posture of a "liability."

Worth more dead than alive? Unlikely. Tupac's star was still on the rise; however, his interests appeared to be shifting slightly, broadening to include a (time-consuming) movie career. Worse yet, Tupac reportedly was putting out feelers for a new record company to produce his albums once he fulfilled his three-album contract with Death Row.

"A few days before he was killed he formally sent a letter telling David Kenner that he no longer could represent him, basically firing him," said Rick Fischbein.

On top of it all, Tupac may have been beginning to make noises about money. Death Row Records claimed that at the time of his death Tupac owed $4.9 million, even though he sold more than $60 million in albums for the label. The money Tupac owed, Death Row claimed, was for services rendered—including Tupac's jail bond money.

But Afeni Shakur has said that her son questioned where all the money was going that his albums were making.

Fischbein claims that Suge would throw money at Tupac periodically to keep him happy. "He asked over and over again for accountings of the things that he did, the monies that came in, and he never got it. When he screamed loud enough, I'm told, they would—someone would bring over a car and say, 'Tupac, here's a Rolls Royce,' and he'd drive it around. Then when he died the family found out none of it was his…"

Also brought into question has been Suge's decision to leave the scene of the shooting and head in a direction away from area hospitals. It's a mistake easily dismissed given the confusion of the moment. Much more interesting is George Kelesis' statement that a planned effort would have required a "crystal ball" because nobody knew the night's plans until the last minute. Suge knew.

But reality takes hold when you consider the actual course of events. It seems inconceivable that Suge would risk putting himself in the path of 13 shots sprayed from a semi-automatic weapon and, in fact, take a bullet in the head to distance himself from Tupac's murder. If he'd known what was coming, you'd think he would have at least worn a bullet-proof vest that night to help ensure his safety. He didn't.

In an interview with Lena Nozizwe on "America's Most Wanted," Suge said as much, calling speculation that he had arranged the shooting ludicrous. "If you look at any interview that Tupac did, if you look at any video, any TV show he did, one thing he always did was praise Death Row. And me and him praised each other. 'Just shoot me in my head, make sure you hit me in my head, so it can look good.' That's crazy."

The theory that Suge had something to do with the death of his top rapper also suffers when you consider Suge's Bloods gang affiliation. Why would he hire a rival Crips member (Las Vegas and Compton police have speculated that Crips were the shooters) to kill Tupac? It doesn't make sense. Though some might argue that it provides the perfect cover, it also creates several additional possibilities for leaks.

Yet another music insider insisted "the trail clearly leads to money. Who benefits?" the source asked. Whatever motive you buy into, "the green" is certainly flowing into the record companies. Tupac's posthumous *Don Killuminati—The*

7-Day Theory (recorded under the pseudonym Makaveli), released six weeks after Tupac's death, sold 664,000 units in
the first week, and 2.5 million copies by April 1997. And
Biggie's posthumous double album, *Life After Death*, sold
690,000 copies in its first week, topping the Billboard charts
with the best first-week sales since the Beatles' double album
Anthology 1 was released in 1995; stores couldn't keep it
stocked.

What's more, the green, if Afeni Shakur is to be believed,
doesn't appear to be flowing out too fast—at least not in her
direction. Afeni contends she is owed money by a music industry that continues to profit from her son's music.

"The entertainment business is a business of prostitu-
tion and thievery, and that was rampant around my son's
talent," Afeni told ABC's "Prime Time Live." "He absolutely
thought he was quite rich and that his family would, you
know, be rich forever. Please remember that my great-grand-
mother was a slave, my grandmother was a sharecropper,
my mother was a factory worker, and I was a legal worker,
do you understand? And so this represents the first time in
our life, in our memory ever, that we have been able to enjoy
the American dream, and that's what Tupac brought to his
family."

But her son owned no assets. Death Row Records, apparently, doled out money and expensive merchandise—cars,
clothes, jewelry, a condo, Afeni's house, cash—to Tupac, but
none of the assets were in his name.

After Tupac died, Afeni arranged to meet with Suge to
settle her son's estate, she said in the same "Prime Time Live"
interview.

"I kept telling Rick [Fischbein], 'We're just going to—
we'll meet with Suge. He'll tell you everything. We'll meet
with him first.' But he didn't even show up."

In December 1996, Afeni filed an infringement lawsuit
against Death Row Records for selling hats, T-shirts, and
sweatshirts connected with Tupac without her permission.
After the lawsuit was filed, Death Row and two companies

that made and distributed the merchandise agreed to a sales moratorium during a hearing in U.S. District Court in Los Angeles. They also promised to deposit potential royalties in a court-monitored account—more than half a million dollars total.

Also, three record producers in March 1997 agreed to delay the release of an album containing two early recordings by Tupac. The move came as a federal judge in Sacramento, California was to rule on a restraining order requested by Afeni Shakur's estate attorney. The three Sacramento-area producers were accused in court documents of "intentionally infringing upon [Tupac's] valuable trademark and publicity rights." The complaint continued, "...[the trio is] profiting from their illicit conversion of songs that he authored and performed in or about 1990, before he became famous, and which belong to Shakur's estate... [The producer's actions] are especially predatory and harmful at this critical point in time, when Shakur's recordings and film appearances are receiving widespread, critical acceptance before a mainstream audience."

Celeste Chulsa, Fischbein's assistant, said Afeni was also seeking rights to previously unseen home videotape of Tupac that was reproduced in the biographical film, *Thug Immortal*. The movie stayed on the *Billboard* top-20 list for several weeks after it was released.

Afeni has also accused Death Row of not giving her any money from her son's estate since his death. She told "Prime Time Live" that Suge had told her at the hospital at her son's deathbed that he would take care of her and her family. When asked if Suge Knight had done that, Afeni answered, "No."

Suge, however, told Lena Nozizwe with Fox's "America's Most Wanted" that Afeni was paid.

"When I was in jail, I gave her a check for $3 million," Suge said. "Plus...I think in four or five months Tupac spent $2.4 million, $2.5 million."

Afeni claims that the $3 million came from Interscope, not Suge, like he promised her.

Besides the money, she described the masters of the 200 songs he recorded as missing. "We don't know where the masters are because we can't get an accounting from Death Row Records," she said.

Suge's attorney, David Kenner, echoed Suge's comments that Death Row had made numerous advances to Tupac and that all of his money had been properly accounted for and paid in a timely manner.

Suge responded to the comments during his final appearance in court. "I'm not mad, but I'm disappointed at Tupac's mother," Suge said during his sentencing speech. "People tell her that the songs I paid for and marketed is her songs. And she made statements saying that he never got any money. I got signed documents where he received over $2.5 million, even before he was supposed to receive money. And beyond all that, when he was incarcerated, I gave his mother $3 million. But when the media gets it, it turns around that I left him for dead, I left him with zero, and that I'm this monster."

"If I was so bad I would have no success," Suge told "Prime Time Live." "I know business. I know how to take my artists and give them superstar status, and [let] them get what they deserve."

Death Row Records countersued after Afeni filed suit against the record company. Death Row claimed Tupac's estate owed the record company $7 million for advances and expenses paid out to Tupac.

Rick Fischbein, who was in the middle of negotiating a settlement on behalf of Tupac's mother with Death Row Records, said a sizable settlement was "imminent."

"We're close to a settlement," Fischbein said in July 1997. "It's a substantial settlement, if it happens. We're certainly all working to try to settle it."

Fischbein also indicated that Death Row had complied on providing an accounting, and that the settlement would not be one lump sum, but a percentage of future sales of Tupac's works.

"We now have an accounting," Fischbein said. "What's

being discussed is not just a single payment. Music is odd in that it doesn't really matter who owns it. The real question is, who gets the money for releasing it or playing it? Owning it is an interesting issue, and it might lead you to get those other rights, but those rights could be separate. These issues are all being discussed."

Police won't commit to saying which of the motive scenarios they believe is most likely. At this point in the investigation, it's still anyone's guess. No one's been arrested, but, as Metro P.D.'s Sgt. Kevin Manning pointed out, no one's been ruled out as a suspect, either.

And no one means no one. One final theory transcends all the others, and implicates the (white) record-company power brokers themselves. Death Row is a black-owned label, but it was financed by white corporate bosses who, it's long been alleged, have profited by exploiting young black men from the ghetto. Use 'em up and throw 'em away is the charge. Tupac Shakur's legal problems alone had become a public-relations nightmare for Death Row's parent corporation. Add to that the public attack on Time Warner over gangsta rap lyrics (Time Warner eventually sold its stake in Interscope), and you have the foundation for a monster conspiracy scenario, the proportions of which dwarf anything previously discussed. Backers of this motive conclude that the murders of Biggie Smalls and Yafeu Fula were crafted to look like gang retaliation to cover tracks.

Writer Kevin Powell said rappers and people in the music business are afraid to speculate about who killed Tupac Shakur. "That's the talk, to be honest, on the streets," he said. "It may have been gang members who pulled the trigger. People believe there may be people behind it, people bigger than gang members. People are afraid to even speculate. It's much more profound than Death Row-Bad Boy. Will we ever know who killed John F. Kennedy or Martin Luther King?"

12

DEAD OR ALIVE?

Even though Tupac Amaru Shakur was gunned down on the streets of Las Vegas in front of at least a hundred people, there are those who refuse to believe that he died from the wounds he suffered that hot September night. "Dead or alive?" is the question that has surfaced again and again concerning the 25-year-old gangsta-rap artist and film star.

Some people, no matter what they hear or see, have chosen to believe Tupac is still alive, sequestered somewhere in Cuba, with sightings in Manhattan, in Arizona (perhaps because of its proximity to Las Vegas), South America, and the Caribbean.

New conspiracy theories claiming Tupac is still alive crop up every day; the World Wide Web is cluttered with their rationalizations. Internet chat rooms are full of dialogue— discussions of whether he did, in fact, pass away.

At the top of the list is the seven-day theory (Tupac was shot on September 7; the numbers in his age, 2-5, add up to seven). Rapper Chuck D, who sings with Public Enemy, has posted "Chuck D's 18 Compelling Reasons Why 2Pac is not Dead" on the Internet. They include the "Makaveli theory"— named after the Italian philosopher Machiavelli, who talked about faking his own death in his works. Tupac was introduced to Machiavelli, including his book *The Prince*, first in high school and later in prison. He would make references to Machiavelli to friends. He named his last album *Makaveli—The 7 Day Theory*—thus the Makaveli and seven-day theory.

Another of Chuck D's "compelling reasons": "The cover of [Tupac's] next album has 2Pac looking like Jesus Christ. Could he be planning a resurrection?"

Chuck D also claims that "Las Vegas is still very much a mob town. No one gets killed on the Strip. You have to pretty much get permission in order for something like this to happen. Who was calling the shots on this one?"

Much of the speculation maintains that medical examiners never did an autopsy, that Tupac's remains weren't cremated as the Davis Mortuary employees claim they were, and that his mother helped him secure a new identity so he could spend the rest of his days out of the limelight in quiet Cuba.

So prominent are the rumors, the police and county officials have been forced to comment on them. Metro Police Lieutenant Wayne Petersen told an Associated Press reporter, "The public believes he staged his own death, for whatever reason."

University Medical Center, where Tupac died, has been deluged with telephone calls. "[The rumor] started probably a couple of weeks after he died," Dale Pugh, a hospital spokesman, said. "It kind of escalated for a while, [then tapered off], but we still get an occasional call. Apparently there's a lot of stuff on the Internet claiming he's still alive, and that may be refueling the rumors.

"I have a son in high school, and he comes home and tells me that he hears Tupac is still alive, that his death was a hoax, and that there was this giant conspiracy to allow him to escape to a more favorable environment. We get calls from people saying they hear the doctor who cared for him has been arrested by the FBI and that the FBI is investigating a conspiracy. It's gotten pretty wild."

"There's the big rumor," said Ron Flud, the Clark County coroner, "that's taken on a life of its own." "TV called me and said, 'We understand that Tupac's not dead.' I told them, 'Well, I can guarantee you he's not down at K-mart with Elvis.'"

Theories aside, the fact is that Tupac *is* dead. Here's the proof.

First, for Tupac to have faked his own death, he would have had to have the cooperation of not only his family, friends, and associates; but of the Clark County Sheriff; the Las Vegas Metropolitan Police Department's patrol, traffic, and bike cops, general assignment and homicide detectives, criminalist investigators, lab technicians, dispatchers, and its public affairs officer; Nevada Highway Patrol troopers and dispatchers; Mercy Ambulance paramedics and dispatchers; Clark County Fire Department firefighters, paramedics, and dispatchers; University Medical Center nurses, doctors, and administrators; the Clark County Coroner and his entire staff of examiners, technicians, and clerks; not to mention reporters and photographers who were on the scene shortly after the shooting. In other words, it would take a conspiracy of epic proportions.

Much of the speculation seems to stem from the air of secretiveness surrounding post-mortem activities. Dale Pugh of University Medical Center, said, "Personally—and I've thought about this a lot—I suspect one of the reasons this still goes around is the media never saw the body leave the hospital, because we didn't want to turn that into some sort of circus. His body went out another exit from the hospital, from the back. That was our decision based on respect for the patient and based on respect for the family and based on the large number of people outside the hospital. We were uncertain as to what might happen and felt that it would be better to take another approach. And we did. As soon as he passed away, we called the media. And as soon as the body was out of the hospital, we again notified the media."

Friends and relatives were allowed to see Tupac in the intensive care unit at University Medical Center, where he lay for six days in a coma until his death on September 13,

1996. After he succumbed to his wounds, Tupac's mother, Afeni, positively identified her son at the hospital. His body was quickly moved to the coroner's office, where an autopsy was performed.

"At a typical autopsy," coroner Ron Flud said, "the people normally in the room are the pathologist, forensic technician, the crime-scene analyst, and the detectives assigned to the case. Look at the number of people who would have had to be involved in this to say that there's some kind of conspiracy or cover-up to facilitate Tupac. I'd never even heard of Tupac [before the shooting]."

The coroner's office in Las Vegas keeps busy. In the fastest-growing city in America, with four to six thousand people moving to the Las Vegas Valley each month and more than thirty million tourists visiting each year, the crime rate has grown nearly as rapidly as the population. Murders in the Las Vegas Valley skyrocketed to an all-time high in 1996; Tupac was one of 207 people murdered in Clark County in that year.

After Tupac's body was taken by a mortuary ambulance to the morgue, a decision was made by both Clark County Coroner Flud, along with a sergeant and two detectives from Homicide, to go ahead with the autopsy that evening. It's not unusual for the process to move quickly in Las Vegas. Examiners often perform autopsies on victims the same day their bodies are brought in, especially in homicide cases. In this case, for security reasons, the coroner didn't want the body to stay in the morgue overnight Too many people knew where the coroner's offices were—around the corner from the hospital where a 24-hour vigil had begun six days earlier following the shooting. Hundreds of people had flocked to the hospital when they heard the news. It was too risky to keep the body until the next day.

Often, homicide detectives follow the coroner to his office so they can witness the autopsy not long after a homicide is committed. Homicide's Sergeant Manning and Detectives Becker and Franks met the ambulance at the coroner's office.

The investigators were in the coroner's examining room as medical examiners performed Tupac's post-mortem exam.

The coroner finished with his examination, autopsy, and coroner's report, and handed over Tupac's body to Davis Mortuary. Davis employees, in turn, cremated Tupac's body, at Afeni Shakur's request. Afeni, after a brief memorial service in Las Vegas with friends and family, returned to her home in Georgia 24 hours after her only son was pronounced dead. The ashes were later scattered over a grassy area in Los Angeles, where Tupac had lived the last years of his life. A small group of family and friends attended the private informal ceremony.

Keith Clinscales, an executive at *Vibe* magazine, issued a statement about the rumors. "Tupac had a huge presence in the community that loved and respected him. [His death] was a human tragedy," he said, calling such rumors cruel and unkind to the Shakur family. "These [rappers] are not comic-book heroes. These are real people."

Tupac did die. Naysayers argue that no photographs showing Tupac's injuries were ever seen. But photos were taken, plenty of them; they just never made it to the press. Any photo of Tupac Shakur in the hospital or in the coroner's office would have fetched a tidy sum from tabloid periodicals, so they were—and still are—kept under lock and key.

Lieutenant Brad Simpson, who oversees Metro's criminalistics unit, which includes the photo lab, said his office's photos of the Tupac Shakur investigation have been locked up.

"The only copies of homicide photos that we keep," he said, "are one set kept with the crime-scene reports and one with homicide.

"There was interest from some of the tabloids in getting some of those photos," Simpson said. "The tabloids offered a lot of money, but they didn't get any photos. They made the offer to the coroner's office. We knew that after the JonBonet Ramsey case in Boulder, Colorado, we had to be careful. We have tighter controls here."

County Coroner Ron Flud was surprised when he received a mysterious call from a man who told the receptionist the call was "personal." Flud took the call in his office.

"The person was being clandestine and said he represented a client who would like to purchase something and would like to meet with me. I told him, 'I don't meet with people.' He said, 'Well, you have some photos.' I knew at that point where he was headed. I stopped him and said, 'No.' At that point, he hung up on me."

Flud said he assumed the man calling him was from a tabloid magazine, but he didn't stay on the phone long enough to find out. He knew about reports of other calls to Metro offering as much as $100,000 for a photo.

"Because of the *Globe* and the *National Enquirer*, [the photos] are under lock and key," Brad Simpson agreed. "It's a policy violation. We'd probably fire the son-of-a bitch too."

Photos were taken during and after Tupac's autopsy by a number of different people. All but one have been accounted for and secured. The one that got away is published in the center photo spread of this book. The photo is explicit. It's not easy to look at. That's because it's real. It's the image of Tupac Shakur lying on a gurney at the morgue, with his chest opened; that's what coroners do when they autopsy bodies. A skull and crossbones tattooed on his right arm are clear and recognizable. The incision doctors made a few days earlier to remove his right lung is visible just above "Thug" on his lower chest. However graphic and gruesome it may be, the photograph in this book should forever dispel any theories that Tupac faked his own death.

Journalist Veronica Chambers, who interviewed Tupac while he was on the set of *Poetic Justice*, wrote in *Esquire*, "Of all the rumors and conspiracy theories I've heard since Tu-pac died, only one has reverberated inside my head: 'I've heard that Tupac isn't really dead.' A friend said, 'Why did they cremate the body right away? In Las Vegas, where they had no family or friends?'

"I shrugged. I make it a point never to argue down conspiracy theories.

"'What I heard is that Afeni has had Tupac's identity changed, and shipped him to Cuba.'

"As I listened to my friend, what surprised me was how my heart leaped at the thought of Tupac alive...

"[On the set] I asked [Tupac] if he didn't think that staying in the Valley, instead of going out and instigating all the trouble he did, would make him live longer. He looked at me as if I were crazy. 'It would be an honor to die in the 'hood,' he said solemnly, as if he were reciting the Pledge of Allegiance. 'Don't let me die in Saudi Arabia. These motherfuckers are rushing with a flag to die on foreign soil, fighting for motherfuckers that don't care about us. I'd rather die in the 'hood, where I get my love. I'm not saying I want to die, but if I got to die, let me die in the line of duty, the duty of the 'hood.' "

Snoop Doggy Dogg, a fellow emcee with Tupac at Death Row Records, perhaps said it best.

"People need to let him rest in peace, let that rumor rest in peace," he told reporters. "Because it's a hard pill to swallow, people don't want to accept it. So they gonna keep that myth or that philosophy goin' on as long as they can because his music lives on and he's a legend, you know what I'm sayin'? When you make legendary music, people don't want to believe you're gone, like Elvis. They keep sayin', 'Elvis ain't dead,' but it's just all about the individual himself. He was a legend, and everybody don't wanna let it go."

13

EULOGY

Since his death, Tupac has been called a black prince, a revolutionary, an icon for Generation X, a hip hop Lazarus, a brotha for black America.

Some see only the tattoos and the jewelry—the body language—as a way of describing him. Or the angry words and the defiant messages. They can't get past his persona.

Still others see Tupac as the young Malcolm X, speaking for young black America, the voice they couldn't find for themselves.

And others see him as the most talented singer ever in the rap-music industry.

To many, Tupac Shakur was a figure of violence, who became a victim of the same violent gang culture he glorified—shot down on the streets of Las Vegas in a gangster-like killing.

Those who knew him best saw him as a force moving toward the truth, cut down before he could mature and reach his full potential, before he had a chance to come into his own. He was young, not yet matured, they said. They felt his anger, his frustration, his pain. They have called him the '90s Elvis, or John Lennon, or Jimi Hendrix, or Jim Morrison, or Sammy Davis Jr., or any other famous singer who was also a symbol of something bigger than himself.

"To me, I feel that my game is strong," Tupac told Tony Patrick. "I feel as though I'm a shining prince, just like Malcolm, and feel that all of us are shining princes, and if we live like shining princes, then whatever we want can be ours." Tupac considered his music spiritual, like the old Negro spirituals. "Except for the fact that I'm not saying, 'We shall overcome,'" he explained. "I'm saying, 'We *are* overcome.'"

Many people believe Tupac was a promising talent who wound up a casualty of a society that destroys African-American youth, males in particular. It's not just a belief among many that the black man in America today is an endangered species. It's based on actual statistics. If the drugs don't get them, the violence will. And if the violence doesn't get them, the cops and the justice system eventually will bring them down.

Writer Kevin Powell elaborated. "There's a perception in the black community that if you're young and black and male, and happen to be making lots of money, you are vulnerable to attacks from the system or the powers that be."

"You know what I think?" E-40, a San Francisco rapper who once recorded with Tupac, asked *Spin* magazine. "Tupac is looking down on us, saying 'Y'all don't know what you're missing up here.' We the ones in hell."

The killing of Tupac Shakur heightened the debate about whether gangsta rap promotes violence or is just a reflection of the ugly mood on the streets. A dark aura of violence looms over the hip-hop music industry. To some, Tupac, with his tattoos that promoted firearms, had it coming. To others, Tupac's songs spoke against the gun culture of the ghetto.

In "Young Niggaz," he sang, "Don't wanna be another statistic out here doin' nothin'/Tryin' to maintain in this dirty game/Keep it real and I will even if it kills me/My young niggaz stay away from these dumb niggaz/Put down the gun and have some fun, nigga."

After Biggie Smalls was shot to death, Quincy Jones, who would have been Tupac's father-in-law had he survived, wrote in *Vibe* magazine, "When will it end? When will the senseless killing of our hip-hop heroes cease? I thought Tupac's death was going to be the end of it, but the psycho-drama keeps going. The murder of Christopher Wallace... is the latest in what is becoming a pathetic string of deaths in and around the rap community. And the speed with which the media turned this unnecessary tragedy into evidence of a 'Rap War,' a 'Slay Revenge,' makes me worry that we haven't heard the last shots ring out yet.

"I love hip hop. To me, it is a kindred spirit to beebop, the music that started my career. But I also know history. The gangster lifestyle that is so often glorified and heralded in this music is not 'keeping it real'; it is fake, not even enter-tainment. A sad farce at best and a grim tragedy at worst.

" 'Real' is being shot five times with 'real' bullets. 'Real' is having a promising life ended at 24 years of age by some-body you might call 'brother.' If that's keeping it real, it is up to all of us to redefine what 'real' means to the Hip Hop Nation...Ultimately, love is real."

In a prepared statement the day after Biggie's death, Quincy Jones said he was "absolutely stunned."

"This death, as well as the death of Tupac Shakur, Eazy-E [from AIDS], Marvin Gaye, and so many more young people who we never hear about, are senseless acts that should never have happened.

"I spent my formative years growing up in 'Gangster Central' on the Southside of Chicago, so I am no stranger to random violence," he said. "If life continues to imitate art this way, it will result in self-inflicted genocide. We all need to reevaluate what our priorities are or else we have nothing to look forward to except more of this madness."

He said he had developed a "close personal relationship" with "the superstar rappers" over the last 10 years. "It's wit-nessing their genius and compassion that makes incidents such as these particularly disturbing to me."

• • •

No formal funeral service was held for the slain rapper. This was at the request of his family, who said he would not have wanted one. In fact, the family told reporters that Tupac had talked about his death and had specifically stated that he didn't want a funeral if he were to die. He told friends when he was in high school that when he died they could snort his ashes and get high off of him. His mother took his ashes home to Georgia to the house Tupac had bought for her (through Death Row). Later, she scattered them over a neighborhood park in L.A.

But spontaneous celebrations of Tupac's life were held all over the country. Friends remembered Tupac at the Civic Center in Atlanta, Georgia., shortly after his death. They called it "Keep Ya Head Up! The Celebration of Tupac Shakur," a three-hour tribute of speeches, poetry reading, dance, and music.

"I know people are sad, but I am here and we are here to celebrate 'Pac and continue on with his spirit," Afeni Shakur said of her son.

Shock G and Money-B, members of Digital Underground where Tupac's professional music career began, issued a statement after Tupac died.

"If you want to mourn, do it for your own personal loss," they said. "Don't mourn for 'Pac. Remember him for his art and don't be sad for his death. 'Pac lived a short, fast, concentrated, and intense life. He lived a 70-year life in 25 years. He went out the way he wanted: in the glitter of the gangsta life, hit record on the charts, new movie in the can, and money in the pocket. All 'Pac wanted was to hear himself on the radio and see himself on the movie screen. He did all that—and more."

Tupac was also mourned at his boyhood church, the House of the Lord Pentecostal Church in Brooklyn, New York, which he joined at age 15 with his mother and sister. Tupac left Brooklyn in his teens, but was still listed as a member of the congregation until his death.

"Who will weep for Tupac Shakur?" the Reverend Herbert Daughtry asked mourners at the memorial service. "I will weep for Tupac. I will weep for all our youth.

"He had the genes, he had the ability. Could we have provided the society that would have made him blossom?"

Daughtry had said that Tupac's self-proclaimed ambition to be a revolutionary against injustice to blacks "was just as real as Martin's and Malcolm's," referring to Martin Luther King and Malcolm X.

"I know that there are those who say he went about it the wrong way, joining the 'gangsta' culture he glorified in his lyrics," Daughtry said. "But it's not for me to judge."

Mikal Gilmore, in a *Rolling Stone* article shortly after Tupac's death, wrote that he suspected "Shakur's death will be cited as justification for yet another campaign against hardcore rap and troublesome lyrics."

"So a man sings about death and killing, and then the man is killed," he wrote. "There is a great temptation for many to view one event as the result of the other. And in Tupac Shakur's case, there are some grounds for this assessment: He did more than sing about violence; he also participated in a fair amount of it. As Shakur himself once said, in words that *Time* magazine appropriated for its headline covering his murder: 'What goes 'round comes 'round.' Still, I think it would be a great disservice to dismiss Shakur's work and life with any quick and glib headline summations. It's like burying the man without hearing him."

The rap writer Kevin Powell seemed to put it in perspective when he eulogized Tupac in the same issue of *Rolling Stone*.

"He was a complex human being; both brilliant and foolish; very funny and deadly serious; friendly and eager to please, but also bad-tempered and prone to violence; a lover of his people and of women but also a peace divider and a convicted sex offender; generous to a fault but also a dangerous gambler when it came to his personal and professional life; incredibly talented but at times frivolously shortsighted. To me, Shakur was the most important solo artist in the history of rap, not because he was the most talented (he wasn't) but because he, more than any other rapper, personified and articulated what it was to be a young black man in America.

"But the demons of Shakur's childhood—the poverty, the sense of displacement, the inconsistent relationship with his mother, the absence of a regular father figure—haunted the rapper all his life. In his song 'Dear Mama,' he sings, 'When I was young, me and my mama had beefs/Seventeen years old, kicked out on the streets.'

"Now that Tupac Shakur is gone, some will charge that it was the music that killed him or that he had it coming because of the choices he made in his life. Those are cop-out, knee-jerk responses. Shakur, in spite of his bad-boy persona, was a product of a post-civil rights, post-Black Panther, post-Ronald Reagan American environment. We may never find out who killed Tupac Shakur, or why he did the things he did and said what he said. All we have left are his music, his films, and his interviews. Shakur lived fast and hard, and he has died fast and hard. And in his own way, he kept it real for a lot of folks who didn't believe that anyone like him (or like themselves) could do anything with his life."

"He's an entertainer, not a gangster. As a person, Tupac is very misunderstood," Keisha Morris, Tupac's ex-wife with whom he remained friends, told *People* magazine while he was in a coma. "I'm still waiting for Tupac to call me," she later told *Rolling Stone* magazine. "I thought he was going to walk out of the hospital just like he did before."

"At the end...you kind of had that feeling he was going to die, according to his preaching," writer Tony Patrick said in *Thug Immortal*. "He seemed to have taken up power and weapons, this posse lifestyle, as his deity. Tupac went from one extreme to the other. There was really no middle ground with him. It was age without maturity, knowledge without wisdom, order turning to chaos. Tupac Shakur should stand as a living testament in the Hip Hop Nation as the pinnacle of greatness achieved, but at the same time, the frailties of human weakness and tragedy."

His stepfather, Mutulu Shakur, wrote a letter, "To My Son," from inside a Florence, Colorado, federal penitentiary the night Tupac died. Excerpts were reprinted on the World Wide Web by Double J Productions.

"I love you whenever, forever. Tupac, so much I needed to say, so much you wanted to say. Many conversations between us within the ether....

"The pain inflicted that scarred your soul but not your spirit gave force to the rebellion. Many couldn't see your dreams or understand your nightmares. How could they, Tupac? I knew your love and understood your passion. But you knew of your beginning and saw your end, racing towards it.

"You taught and fought through your songs and deeds. Ratt-tatt-tatt of words penetrating the contradiction of our existence...

"Who cares? We cared, Tupac. The Shakurs have been guided by struggle, prepared or not, whenever, forever. We've exposed our existence, naked from fear, to those who would hear the positive. Who would witness the stress, wear and tear of this lonely path? You couldn't have evaded the effect or the changes. You inherited it; it was in your genes.

"Friday the 13th didn't mean a thing. Life is for living and dying well... You understand the pain of disappointment in the ones we love. You pushed so many away. Burnt so many bridges so they wouldn't follow you into battles against the demons you were facing. Knowing well to what lengths you would go. This battlefield of reality is littered with many meaningless casualties.

"You never yelled out, 'Somebody, save me!' You only asked for your soul to be free, whenever, forever. You told us to keep our head up, knowing the pain was coming. Knowing to look for the strength in the heavens. Set your soul free, Tupac Amaru.

"The victories—we will teach your mission. We are thankful for you. We love you, Tupac Shakur. We ain't mad at you. We'll be better because of you.

"So now I give you my tears so I might assimilate your loss and I can live on in peace.

"Knowing I will feed your spirit with my unconditional love, knowing you will need it on your next journey. May Allah bless you for your deeds and forgive your errors. Tupac, come to me and give me strength.

Love always,

Your father, friend, comrade, Mutulu."

Billy Garland, Tupac's real father, said in an exclusive interview with Kevin Powell for *Rolling Stone* magazine that his son didn't deserve to be criticized.

"My son is dead, and he don't deserve to be talked about like some common criminal," Garland said. "He wasn't perfect, but he did do some great things in a little bit of time."

And, finally, Tupac Shakur's mother Afeni spoke about her only son.

"Tupac has always been the person who's made up the game—always," she told *Vibe* magazine before his death and after one of Tupac's many court arraignments. "He would have make-believe singing groups, and he would be Prince, or Ralph in New Edition. He was always the lead."

And after his death, she told a *Vanity Fair* reporter, "From the moment he was born, I measured his life in five-year periods. When he was 5, I was so grateful. When he was 10, I thanked God he was 10. Fifteen, 20, 25. I was always amazed he'd survived. He was a gift."

The killing of Tupac Shakur remains unsolved.

APPENDIX

Official Coroner's Report

Case No. 96-03854

REPORT OF INVESTIGATION
OFFICE OF THE CORONER MEDICAL EXAMINER, CLARK COUNTY, NEVADA
1704 Pinto Lane, Las Vegas, Nevada 89106

DECEDENT SHAKUR, TUPAC A. **AKA** LESANE PARISH CROOKS **Status** S **DOB** 06/16/1971
Residence Address 8489 W. 3RD ST., STE. 1038, LOS ANGELES, CA 90048
Tel No. (213) 653-3515 **Desc: Sex** M **Race** N **Age** 25 **SS #** 546-47-8539 **Height** 72.00
Weight 215.00 **Hair** BROWN **Eyes** BROWN

Scars/Tattoos & Other identifying features
TATTOOS: SKULL - RIGHT SHOULDER, THUGLIFE - STOMACH, NUMEROUS OTHER TATTOOS ON BODY.
Rigor Mortis NONE **Livor Mortis** NONE **Decomposed?** No
Clothing NONE
Drugs & Medications
NONE NOTED

Occupation RAP SINGER **Employed by** EUPHANASIA
Agency Reporting UNIVERSITY MEDICAL CENTER **Date & Time Reported** 09/13/96 16:15
Location of body UMC TRAUMA ICU
Type of Death V **At Work:** N

CIRCUMSTANCES	DATE	TIME
Reported to Agency by		
Name & Address		
Last Seen Alive by		
Name & Address		
Found Dead by		
Name & Address		
Pronounced Dead by	09/13/96	16:03
Name & Address	DR. LOVETT	
Body Viewed by	09/13/96	16:15
Name & Address	ED BROWN, CCCME	
Identified by	09/13/96	17:00
How Identified	VIEWING	
Name & Address	AFENI SHAKUR, MOTHER	
Witnesses		

Law Enforcement Agency LVMPD **Event #** 960907-2063
Officers SGT. MANNING, SGT. ANDERSEN
OFC. DENSLEY P#3577, OFC. DEBECKER P#3917, CSA LEMASTER
Property Receipt # 50389
In Custody of NO PROPERTY TAKEN
CUSTODY OF BODY: Removed by DAVIS **To** CCCME
Driver SONNY THOMAS
Assisted by TROY FARRELL
Requested by FAMILY

DEATH NOTIFICATION
N.O.K. AFENI SHAKUR **Relationship** MOTHER
Address 883 RAYS ROAD, STONE MTN., GA 30083 **Tel No.** (404) 508-8599
Other #1 **Relationship**
Address **Tel No.**
Other #2 **Relationship**
Address **Tel No.**
Means PERSONAL CONTACT AT THE HOSPITAL
Notification Made by ED BROWN, CCCME **Date** 09/13/96 **Time** 17:00

VEHICULAR DEATHS: Deceased was **Seat Location**
Vehicle **Lic No** **State**
Accident location **Date** **Time**
SAFETY EQUIPMENT USED: Seat belt **point** **Air bag** **Other**

ABOUT THE AUTHOR

Cathy Scott is a full-time police reporter for the *Las Vegas Sun*. A reporter for over a decade, Scott has received more than a dozen journalism awards. Her articles have appeared in the *Los Angeles Times* and the *New York Times*. Scott covered the Los Angeles riots, Operation Restore Hope in Somalia, and the Republic of Panama's drug interdiction program. She holds a bachelor of science degree from the University of Redlands.